Table of Contents

Dedications	Page 2
Introduction	Page 3
Caution: Forks Ahead	Page 6
Decisions, Decisions	Page 11
Trouble Is Brewing	Page 15
Traveling an Unlit Path	Page 21
Unfamiliar Territory	Page 33
One Road Leads to Another	Page 38
Starting Over in a New Place	Page 44
The Temporary U-Turn	Page 47
On the Road Again	Page 52
Feeling Like a Foreigner	Page 55
Caught Up in Madness	Page 60
The Road to Discovery	Page 64
No Denying the Truth	Page 71
Recognizing The Wrong Direction	Page 77
On Again, Off Again	Page 83
Time to Turn Around for Good	Page 86
Final Thoughts	Page 89
Personal Note	Page 105

Dedications

I dedicate this book to every person that may end up holding it in their hands. You found it for a reason. May God bring you the truest peace and comfort that only He can provide.

To my true friends and family that have stood by me when everyone else was gone: Thank you for loving me *unconditionally*.

To my three sons: I will always love you with *all* of my heart. Life will ultimately bring you challenges of your own. I will pray faithfully that when you approach your own "forks-in-the-road" that you have the wisdom and courage to make good, sound decisions that will lead you to sunny places.

To my husband: Thank you for proving to me that even bad decisions don't have to plague your life forever. Forgiveness, respect, and love can be just around the corner if you just wait on God.

Most of all, I would like to express my deepest thanks to the one that bought my pardon with His blood and gave me grace and mercy that I didn't deserve. Had it not been for my deep belief that there was a God waiting nearby who wouldn't let me fall into the abyss; who would never leave me, I truly don't know where I would be today.

Introduction

I guess everybody has skeletons in their closet, and I'm no different. This book is filled with a lot of things that were very difficult to write. It made me relive a lot of memories that I've tried very hard to push aside. It was emotionally draining. Sometimes the painful truths were more than I wanted to bear. You might be wondering why in the world I would want to "air my dirty laundry" for the world to see considering there are probably a lot of people that would love to get their hands on it just to judge me or to break down my moral character. I tell my story only to help others. Names have been changed to protect the privacy of the real-life characters of my story; however, as for myself, I'm not really concerned about what people will think of me anymore. I have a burning desire in my heart to help those out there that may be where I once was; out there hurting or feeling like there's no hope for them. They need to know that they are worthy of a life of joy. I look back at my past with a different perspective now. I choose to look at my past decisions as learning experiences. Until I began to see them as such, they were just regrets. I remember feeling like I didn't deserve God's forgiveness, because I felt like I wasn't worthy to talk to him or ask him for help simply because I'd failed him many times. I remember feeling humiliation and shame that I hadn't made different choices; better choices.

I know what it's like to want to bury your head in the sand and hide your face from the world. Had it not been for a handful of people who withheld judgment and showed me love in the middle of the storm that thrashed all around me; who encouraged me to seek God's help and let Him love me in spite of my shortcomings; I just don't know how I would have found the courage to walk towards a better life. I grew up thinking that God's watchful eye was always on me and that He was just waiting for a reason to bring down the hammer, strike me with lightening, or punish me. Now I know different. God does not like to see us hurt any more than we want to see our own kids hurt or struggle. He loves us more than our earthly parents. He loves us with a kind of love that we simply are not able to comprehend. No matter what you've done, where you've been, or what you're going through, believe me when I say that you *can* trust Him. When it seems He is far away, He is simply waiting for you to let Him have control.

I want to inspire you to rise above the pain and take a walk towards the light at the end of the tunnel. I want you to know that you don't deserve to live in an abusive situation. I want you to see that you have more power inside of you than you think. I want to prove to you that you can still go on when life has tossed you about and slammed you into a brick wall a few times. I want you to know that when you feel you are alone and that there is no one to turn to; there is a friend that will stick closer to you than a brother (*Proverbs 18:24, Holy Bible*). I want you to look inside of yourself, figure out your passion and purpose, and know that nothing is impossible. I want to assure you that as soon as you make a solid decision not to be a victim, you won't be! Most of all, I want you to realize that you have choices: big choices, little choices, and each one of them leads you somewhere. Each one affects your life in more ways than you know, and they also affect the lives of others connected to you. You cannot blame anyone else for the path you walk now. You took a walk in that direction, whether you want to make excuses for how you got there or not. When I became willing to accept the consequences of each of my actions and own them, I took back my power to be able to change my situation. As you read these pages, I hope you get the message that I am trying to send and I hope you find the strength to do what you must do when you find yourself at a Fork-in-the-Road. What you do at each one *really* matters! Not just for you, but for those connected to you too.

Caution: Forks Ahead!

Every person happens upon them once in a while during the course of his or her life. It's inevitable. I like to call them "forks-in-the-road". Everyone's heard the expression, but I firmly believe in these forks and that they serve a purpose in the lives of all who encounter them. I believe that forks-in-the-road are placed in our paths with great care, to teach us something very valuable. Some people say they've made a lot of mistakes. I used to say that, however that was long before I became the person I am today and matured to the point that I now know better. Personally, I am convinced that there is a difference between a "mistake" and a "bad decision".

A mistake means that you didn't intend on doing something. Once you consciously make a decision to act on something, it's no longer a "mistake". It's a bad decision. I *do* believe that everything happens for a reason. We all have learning experiences, and some of them are more painful than others. I call the more painful ones "growing pains". Again, I repeat: In life decisions, I really don't buy into the whole "mistakes" theory in entirety.

Once you cross the threshold of action even though you know something is not right, it's a **bad decision**; and I've made my fair share of them. I used to believe that when you get to those places in life that you find yourself at a proverbial "fork-in-the-road" needing to make a decision on which way to go, that the two choices led to a "right" or "wrong" decision. Whatever decision you made would invoke good or bad consequences, was the general idea. While I do believe that there is a clear "right" and a clear "wrong", I also believe that even if you choose the wrong path, you are still redeemable. I still believe that there is a sequence of events set up for each choice (good decision or bad decision) and depending on the path you decide to take, the lesson may be more or less painful. The knowledge you gain from one learning experience may cost you more than another, but your decision to enter either path sends the dominoes of life falling in a pattern specifically designed for that particular fork-in-the-road. Unfortunately, your decision might affect more than just your journey. It can impact others connected to you as well (some of the people you love most), and we don't always choose the easiest or most logical path. Sometimes we choose the road less traveled. Sometimes we have to do it *our* way. Often times it leaves others scratching their heads or judging us for what they see as a "no-brainer", especially if they see it as a moral dilemma and with good reason when you're actually thinking rationally, and clearly. The problem with that is that we don't always act according to what makes good sense. Sometimes we are *not* thinking so clearly. Sometimes we let feelings override our senses, and feelings can be very deceptive depending on what state of mind you are in at the time.

   I knew that if I wrote a book about this portion of my life, it would be full of twists and turns with plenty of dark places. Some of you will be shocked, appalled, bewildered, and/or puzzled. Some of you will shake your head in disbelief and maybe even say, "I would never do that" or wonder what in the world I must have been thinking. Trust me when I say, looking back even I wonder what I must have been thinking! I have learned one lesson in life that I will never again need to repeat. *By the grace of God*, I will *never* say what I would or wouldn't do in any given situation, nor cast judgement on others. Depending on what a person is going through, how or where he/she grew up and/or under what conditions, the person's current mental or emotional stability, and all of the many circumstances surrounding him or her; there's just no way to say what anyone would or should do in any given situation. It is something as unique and individual as the person. You can't truly say with 100% accuracy what you would do until you are actually faced with the very exact situation, governed by the very same factors as the person who actually experienced it. Unless you've walked every step of that person's life in his or her shoes, you can't truly say one way or the other. No one can honestly say which path they would have chosen in your place, because no one can say they've experienced every single experience that you have experienced and we are all as unique as fingerprints. Decisions are not always simple, nor do I believe that they are meant to be seen as black or white all of the time. There are gray areas that we should be paying much more attention to than we do. Others may *think* they know what they would have done, or could have done, but the fact is there is no way they can possibly know. They don't know the details of your life plan. They don't know what shaped you into a "bad decision-maker", or any of the other things in life that shaped who you became. Only God knows your plan, and it's up to each and every one of us to try to figure it out. The Bible would be a good roadmap, but even if you grew up as a Christian you may not use that valuable guide when you most need it! No one knows the circumstances surrounding you as you approached each fork-in-the-road, or what led you to your final decision. They don't know your state of mind when you made that decision. They don't know what was going on in your life at the time or what you'd been thru up to that point. They don't know what lessons that you specifically were put here to learn. I have learned that if not for the grace of God, I am prone to make "bad decisions" over and over again. I don't think there's a person alive that would be able to honestly say they have never regretted a decision they made, or that they don't harbor something inside that they would be horrified to know they had to expose. If there is, I need to meet that person! I have walked some very rocky roads in life. I've often wondered why I was chosen to walk down that thorny path. Why me? After experiencing several life-changing events, I finally had to ask myself, "Why not me?

In Matthew 5:45 of the Holy Bible it states that it "rains on the just and the unjust". I find that statement to be true. Bad things sometimes happen to good people. Good people sometimes make bad decisions. Sometimes I made it "rain" on myself! I have lived my share of chaotic times; some of it due to my own decisions or choices, and some of it fate, destiny, or what I call inevitable "learning experiences". Looking back, I can see very specific times when I approached what I refer to as "forks-in-the-road".

If you go to any nice eat-in restaurant, when they arrange your silverware, you will see two forks. Usually, table settings will consist of a knife, a spoon, and two forks: one large fork and one smaller fork. Imagine not being used to seeing those forks, because you've never been to a fine dining restaurant and you've never had a mentor to try to teach you about each one. You're not really sure which one to choose. Technically, you can eat with either fork. However, one is really intended for your main course, and the other for your beginning salad. Such is life; two forks, one decision with a 50/50 chance of getting it right.

Which will it be? It is up to you to make the choice, and either way the fork you choose matters as it will lead you to a specific place. Hind sight, they say, is 20/20. I can look back at several "forks" in my life and see where my decisions led me to a completely different place than I'd likely have landed had I chosen the alternate direction. I believe the lessons I learned along the way (even the tough ones where I didn't get the opportunity to make my own decisions) were imperative for my spiritual and emotional growth. I simply would not be the same person today had not experienced the things I've experienced. I want to talk about the forks I encountered during my lifetime, and where they led me. It is my hope that you will get the point that every path you trod sets the dominoes of your life falling in a certain direction. Every fork that you choose has an impact on the rest of your life one way or another, and will likely impact those connected to you as well. Unfortunately, I found this out the hard way.

Decisions, Decisions

I decided to start with the very first conscious decision I ever made that I can remember; my very first fork-in-the-road. I was eighteen years old. I had been dating a boy I'll call "Jay" on and off for my four years of high school, starting around the age of fifteen. I was completely and utterly in love with Jay. He was my first love. In fact, we'd talked about someday getting married, having kids, a dog and the white picket fence. We did everything together. I trusted him, which was hard for me to do coming from a very dysfunctional home. A lot happened in that war called "home", but that's a story for another time.

The first break up with Jay was very hard for me. He'd "cheated" on me with a girl at a church youth camp. He got caught kissing behind one of the buildings. It had just so happened I'd gone to the closing night because they made it part of revival. They had something they called "kangaroo court" in which camp attendees who got caught doing something wrong were put to trial and given their just punishments. I was so excited to see Jay, because I hadn't seen him all week long. I never suspected anything bad would happen. I mean, after all, I had a Christian boyfriend. I would have never believed he could hurt me. He waved and smiled and took his place on a bench close to the front for the final campers' ceremonies. I was about to be introduced to my very first, crushing heartbreak. Imagine my shock when Jay was one of the accused! There I was, with all of his friends in attendance (who knew me and also knew that we were a couple), when they announced that Jay got caught kissing one of the girls behind a building. It was funny to everyone else (even he was laughing about it), but it wasn't the least bit funny to me. I felt horrified; absolutely humiliated. I felt my face flash red. I had a huge lump in my throat as I tried to fight back the tears that wanted to fall. I had to sit through the rest of that service, because my mother was there for the camp-meeting service and she wanted to hear the preacher that night. I couldn't wait until it was over. I needed out of there so badly.

I finally let out my hurt and anguish in the car on the way home. Jay hadn't even looked my way after his "sentencing". He was laughing through it all as if he was oblivious to what it felt like to be me. It was as if I didn't exist to him at all that night. Of course, my mother reminded me that this was my first boyfriend and that this kind of thing happens and that I'd get over it. To me, it felt like I lost a piece of myself. After Jay got out of youth camp, he called me to ask what I was up to as if nothing had ever happened. He'd known that I was going to be there that night. I'd told him earlier in the week since my mother wanted to go to the camp-meeting service that night. When he finally called me after camp was over, I listened for a few minutes in disbelief (fuming the entire time) that he acted like nothing was out of the norm. I was shocked that he didn't have anything to say about that night and what happened. I listened as long as I could until I finally snapped. I unloaded on him with all four barrels. I let him know that I had a problem with the way I was treated.

After his "girlfriend" that he'd had at the camp was gone he just seemed to become more and more mesmerized by other females. He was constantly chasing someone else. I broke up with him after months of the same kinds of betrayals, and I found myself a new boyfriend. Once the excitement of all of the attention he was getting was gone, Jay wanted to get back together. After all, he said, "We've been together almost the entire four years of high school". Well, I didn't want a repeat with him. Even though the new boyfriend and I had broken up by the time Jay had this sudden epiphany, other boys had started showing an interest in me during my senior year of high school and I had no desire to be hurt by him again. I no longer trusted a word he said. Supposedly, it hurt him badly that his genuine regret and apology was rejected. Maybe that was his lesson to learn. But either way, Jay got to see exactly what it was like to be the one on the receiving end of getting tossed aside for someone "better".

   I went on dating other people, though not exclusively. Right before high school graduation, Jay called me unexpectedly. He was going into the military, and he wanted to see if we could work things out since he was much more mature and knew what he really wanted. He missed me. He wanted to try again. I had a decision to make, because honestly, I did still care for Jay. It was my first fork- in-the-road leading me into the beginning of my adult life. Ultimately, I decided I didn't want to take a risk of going through similar experiences with Jay, and having to worry about what he was up to behind my back all of the time. My trust in him was just not there. So, I wished him well and told him I wasn't really interested. He went off with the military and ended up marrying one of the very girls he was "chasing" while he was dating me a year or so after that. That sent a clear message to me that he didn't really care as much about me as he said he did. But they are still together today. They have three beautiful children, and some grandchildren now and I truly hope life is good for them. I did get an apology from Jay later in life. He wanted me to know how sorry he was for "being a jerk" and hurting me. He said he was a young, dumb boy. I could have told him to "buzz off", but instead, I told him not to worry about it. That was a long time ago, and not one of us can say we haven't regretted things we've done. He moved on and so did I. Now back to the story, Jay found a beautiful girl to marry, and I carried on with my own life. Basically existing. Just a lost, broken soul.

    As soon as I turned 18 years old, I left the house I lived in with my mother and my adoptive father (who had married my mother when I was 2 years old) to escape his yelling, demeaning, and abusive behavior among other things. I moved in with an aunt (my mother's sister) who had a daughter one year younger than me, only to end up moving out about two months later after some tension that once again left me feeling like I *"just didn't belong"* the same as always. It wasn't that I was asked to leave, but some things were said that made me feel like they had grown tired of me being there, so I just chose to go. I'd always felt like a misfit no matter where I was, and this was no different. It wasn't anything they did, really, though I did feel like I 'd worn out my welcome there. It was mostly me feeling like I'd always felt: like an **outsider**. I had graduated, I had no car or job, and I was desperately trying to find my way. I found something alright, but not something that made life any better for me. Looking back, it's almost like I was in some sort of self-destruct mode from the start. I was messed up in ways I never truly understood until much later.

Trouble is Brewing

My second fork came not very long after I wandered down the road from the first one. Here I was eighteen years old, when I met a Navy man through a mutual friend. "Mitchell" was almost five years older than me. He was stationed at a base near my home town. He hadn't been out of his own serious relationship long. He had broken things off with his fiancé and sent her back to California recently. He lived not even ten minutes from my family's home. I found him rather obnoxious at first and somewhat cocky, but at the same time there was also something that I found alluring about him. Maybe it was the fact that I didn't have anyone chasing me at the time. Maybe it was because I really needed to feel wanted. I began to date him pretty often. Shortly thereafter, a very good friend of mine confessed to having feelings for me. I really didn't want to be a "cheater" having gone through heartbreak a time or two with Jay, but I did find myself teetering on "what ifs" and hanging out with my friend "Adam" a lot more. All the while, I was asking myself if I really was interested in Adam beyond friendship. We would be graduating together. I entertained the idea, but quickly decided that Adam was not really going to be any more to me than a friend. Adam had a few problems with marihuana and hung out with the wrong kinds of people; all of which turned me off to any kind of serious relationship with him. So, I began to focus more on Mitchell. Later in life (in his 20's), Adam ended up committing suicide. I often wonder if my "rejection" played a part in that. Either way, I sadly lost a good friend. It just made me feel lonelier than I already was most of my life, and it reinforced that old familiar feeling that I never fit in with the regular crowd; that I never "belonged" no matter where I went.

Still, there was something "commanding" about Mitchell's personality and he had my attention for sure. Looking back, maybe it was because he was a man in "uniform" (Navy), or maybe it was because he showed interest, period. But I still remember the night we first became intimate. He'd asked me if I was sure if I wanted to "do this". I was smitten by that point, with the idea of having a relationship and someone to finally love me; to finally want me. I knew it wasn't "right" to be intimate outside of wedlock, because I'd grown up in a religion that taught us it was wrong according to the Bible. I did feel a conviction about it. I wasn't sure about anything really at that time, because some things about Mitchell made me raise an eyebrow of concern a time or two, but one thing led to another and I just continued down the same path with him, desperately wanting to be loved. By then I'd left my aunt's house and moved in with a cousin. I was pretty messed up emotionally. My adoptive father was not a very loving man; in fact, he was just the opposite and I couldn't wait to get out of the house when I'd left. I weighed my options. I was fresh out of high school. I had only worked a few part-time jobs. I was unemployed, had no car, and **now** after dating Mitchell for only a brief time, I found myself **pregnant**. SO... *What in the world was I going to do?*

Mitchell asked me if I wanted to get married. Honestly, I didn't feel I had a lot of choices. As soon as I told my mother that I was pregnant, she told me that they could not afford to help me with a baby, but I knew that really came from my step-father, and I already knew that no help would be offered. She also told me that the relationship would never work, because we didn't have the same values or belief system. In my mind I was thinking: This man could be shipped out and my baby would never know his father, not to mention that with my upbringing the moral and right thing to do was to get married. So, three months after I met

Mitchell, we were married. I walked down the aisle (nauseous as could be) asking myself if this was really the right thing to do. I just wasn't sure about it at all, and looking back, it really wasn't the time to make a life-changing decision feeling a hesitation like that. A person should be excited on wedding day, but regardless, Mitchell and I somehow made it through all of that only for me to give birth to a very sick baby. We almost lost our firstborn son. Thus, this created more challenges for us as a newly married couple, and lots of raw emotions ensued. Time heals most wounds, so within two years of the birth of my first son, I found myself wanting another baby. Mitchell was hesitant, but my oldest son was almost two years old and I didn't want my children to be too far apart. I wanted them to be able to relate to each other. Twenty-five months after the birth of my son, we became parents to a second son. It felt really good. Life seemed to be going a little smoother than before, and I felt like I was finally learning more about how to be a better wife and mother. Or so I thought.

This is probably a good time to mention "unplanned events". There are forks-in-the-road where you actually get to make a decision as to which path to take, and then there are "events". My second son was six months old when I found out that I was a month pregnant with yet a third child, two and a half years into my new marriage. This was totally unexpected, though I must say that we were not as faithful as we should have been when it comes to birth control. Fifteen months after the birth of my second son, my third son joined our family. I was a very young mother of three not at all prepared for this much responsibility, not really having the life skills to know what I was doing, and life got really tough after that. I loved my boys more than anything, but at times it could be overwhelming; **very** overwhelming to someone with so little experience and not the best examples to follow. Problems grew in every direction.

   Mitchell ended up deciding to get out of the Navy when his enlistment came up again. This decision was largely influenced by me, a young woman who was not ready to be left alone with three children under the age of three for extended periods of time. Sometimes our decisions or desires impact other people in our lives as well. I'm sure there have been plenty of times when Mitchell wonders why he ever got out of the military he loved so much just for me. I still sometimes feel bad about that, but I did reach out to him one day and tell him that I realize I should have been more supportive and I wasn't, and I was sorry for that and so much more. At any rate, to avoid having sea duty and being away from all of us Mitchell ended up finding a job in the restaurant business. He worked very long hours. A time or two he even spent the night at the workplace, which caused suspicions on my part. I was always at home by myself with our babies. I sometimes wondered if he really was just spending the night at work, or what else he may be doing. I never could feel secure in any relationship. It put a lot of pressure on our marriage, which he didn't seem all that concerned about to me, and I eventually I gave him an ultimatum. I couldn't deal with him never being at home, and I couldn't deal with being what felt like "a single parent" to three. As a result, Mitchell ended up unemployed, because I could not tolerate his work schedule and he quit that job to try to find something that would allow him to be home a little more. Mitchell then found another job making $ 5.50 per hour at a fabricating company thanks to a gentleman at church helping him get a job, and he worked his rear off to keep our family afloat. That line of work was a lot more physical, but he did get to be home more. To this day, I'm not sure how we made it. But God!

Eventually, Mitchell worked his way up to making great money as a fitter/welder. Within a few years, we were able to get out of the little shack we rented and buy a home. Life seemed pretty good for us. Life **was** good for us, except for one thing. I had always felt a disconnection between us that really never got better with time. Mitchell wasn't overtly affectionate. We went through the normal motions, but on a more intimate, emotional level, something was wrong. We weren't as close as I wanted to be in our marriage. I didn't feel that he was "plugged into" the relationship. I began trying to talk to him about it rather frequently, which usually left us both frustrated and ended up with me crying. I desperately wanted to feel wanted and *needed*. I realize now that part of the problem was that I was approaching my mid-twenties when every woman begins to wonder if she's where she's supposed to be, what her purpose is, and if she's truly loved and wanted which can be a volatile frame of mind. Not to mention, he made it clear that if I wasn't happy, he could live with or without me (probably due to the frustration of it all) which made me feel completely disposable to him. That's **not** what I needed to hear and definitely wasn't what I was looking for in a relationship.

After three children and sitting idle and eating to drown my emotions, I had put on a large amount of weight, and I was very depressed. Mitchell wasn't well equipped to deal with it, and it didn't help me that he didn't seem to care. He finally reached a point where he just didn't want to engage in the discussions anymore. He'd say he was sleepy, and he'd walk away and go to bed and leave me to wallow in my tears. We began to argue. Mitchell somewhat retreated and got to a point that he just wouldn't talk about it at all. I guess avoidance was better than the stress for him. I became more and more resentful, and less and less concerned about fixing whatever was wrong in my marriage. In my mind, if Mitchell wasn't listening, I might as well give up trying to be heard. My "knight in shining armor" was *not* coming to my rescue.

I had been very active in the church during my youth and into my adulthood. My mother had found a church she felt comfortable in and we'd been going there since I was only five years old. It was a place I could take my children, and it was a place where I could find comfort in a higher power. I had been singing in the church since I was a very young five-year-old. By now, I was twenty-six years old and church was my home away from home. It was my only escape from the misery I felt inside. The only time we weren't stuck in that house with no one around. The boys and I went to church every Sunday and every Wednesday. Sometimes, the boys would go to other programs for the children. Mitchell rarely went with me. In fact, it was a chore to get him to go. I begged, pleaded, cried, and even tried laying guilt trips on him. Nothing worked. First off, I went to an Assembly of God church and he didn't really understand my religion with people "speaking in tongues" there, etc. Secondly, it just wasn't his thing. He couldn't have cared less about going. For me, it seemed like no matter what the subject matter; if it was important to me, it just didn't seem to be important to Mitchell. It caused more division between us. I couldn't connect with him on any level. His once-in-a-blue-moon church trips finally dwindled down to none at all. I finally stopped caring and stopped asking him to go. That's when I approached the next "fork" that would lead me to a very dark place.

Traveling an Unlit Path

During the time Mitchell and I were becoming estranged from one another in the strongest sense of the word, Thomas, a man I'd known for many years from church and was somewhat of a childhood friend called me one day at work (I had started a job when my youngest child started school at four years of age to help with our day-to-day expenses). I was kind of taken by surprise that Thomas called, but he began asking me what I thought about what was going on in the church concerning our preacher and it made sense that he was just looking for my opinion. Our current pastor had not made many friends in the congregation and people had turned against him. Now the church wanted to vote him out. Thomas and I chatted about that and that started our conversations. Thomas continued to call once in a while after that to make small talk, or to ask me how I was doing. I began confiding in him about my home life. To me, he was a childhood friend that we grew up with so the red flag just didn't wave for me. I expressed that I wasn't sure if I was happy anymore, and talked about how little my husband had to do with me or my life. He, in return, admitted that he was not fully connected with his wife either. His wife rarely came to church with him, and with Mitchell not accompanying me, it was a recipe for trouble. Thomas and I could commiserate with each other. In my mind, I really thought I was just confiding in a friend. Thomas wasn't sure what his next move would be, but he wasn't happy and didn't know how to change any of it without causing arguments or fights at home. We began trying to be there for one another, as longtime friends and confidants. Honestly, at that point it was just an innocent friendship. But, looking back to that day, I can see now that it was truly playing with fire on both our parts. We'd stand out in the parking lot after church and talk about things or just make small talk for a little while to escape from the reality waiting for us on the home front, and then we would go home. I should have seen it coming, but I didn't. I *honestly* thought I was just innocently being there for a friend and he was being there for me. I mean we'd known each other our whole lives. One night, I mentioned that I was going to go into town to look at an electric piano keyboard. He asked if he could ride with me. Apparently, his wife was not going to be home when he got there anyway, and he was just looking to kill time. I said "Okay, sure" oblivious to the big imaginary warning sign that was glaring before me like a neon sign (*Hello, Tracey?!?!?!*), and off we went downtown looking for my equipment.

That night, another fork came into view. It probably had flashing lights on it on the treacherous path I was about to go down, but I chose not to see them. On our way back towards home, he sat a little closer. It was a little awkward for me, but it was someone showing kindness and tenderness and it had been a long time I'd had that. Thomas laid his head on my shoulder and told me that he'd always found me to be a funny, beautiful girl. He told me that when he and my younger brother used to hang out, that he kind of had a crush on me. He admitted that he'd always had some feelings for me, and that when I'd gotten married to Mitchell, he was a little disappointed. He said that he'd always wanted to go out with me, but never had the nerve to ask, because I always seemed to have a boyfriend. That's true, because I was *always* looking for someone to fill that void inside of me. I was *always* looking for someone that would just love me. When you get two people together that aren't exactly happy where their lives are, trouble is surely on the way. Before I knew what happened, he kissed me. From there it went from bad to worse. I *could* have chosen to do the right thing, but I didn't even resist, and I believe it's because I was so hungry for attention for most of my life that I didn't want it to end. I'd lost a lot of weight by that time, and it seemed like my husband still didn't really "see me", much less listen to me. I found myself looking forward to seeing Thomas. He called me all of the time now, and one day Thomas even showed up at my house when Mitchell had gone out of town with our boys to see his mother. I was shocked that he'd do that, but I was enjoying the attention way too much to care. I did feel guilty from time to time, but it was totally overshadowed by the fact that I had someone who was actually interested in *me*. He asked if he could stay for the night so we could talk and I wouldn't have to be alone. I agreed. In my mind I'm thinking there were extra rooms there, so why not? I knew it was wrong, but I just didn't seem to have the wherewithal to stop myself. I wanted so badly to be wanted. Wrong or right, I was choosing my path. This path started the spiral down into a darkness I should not ever have entertained and highly underestimated. I actually lay blame on myself more than him, because I had the option to stop it at any time, and I *could have*, but simply didn't do it.

    I only tell this story now, because I know it's necessary. I know someone out there might be teetering on the verge of the very same type of decision. You **and** the innocent people that you love are sure to get hurt. If you are a guilty party to this kind of betrayal, you are sure to live with regret that you will never forget or outlive. Put simply: You can run away from a lot of things, but you cannot run from yourself. Wherever you go…there you will be! Even if you wanted to forget, there are those that will not let you years and years down the road. It's just not worth it. You will lose part of your soul and almost all of your self-worth. I used to think I would never fall to such depths. I guess I thought I was above it. I was raised in church from the age of five, and I hate to say it, but I had often judged people who did these types of things or even far less. Most people I knew in church were full of judgment. I still sometimes hear people say, "I'm not judging; I'm just telling the truth." The truth is, if you are condemning another human being, you are judging that person. Let's just call it what it is, and it is what it is! Nowadays, I try my best to never do that nor be a part of it. Because I learned something: "Except for the grace of God, there go I" (John Bradford). To be weak in the flesh is nothing new, but it is amazing to me that people still believe they are above that temptation just because they were raised in church or "taught better than that". Now, here I was, Little Miss Churchgoer, about to become the judged and rightfully so if you're going on the "guilt factor".

Thomas and I became involved romantically and emotionally, and both of us knew better. We were both married. To make it much worse, I was a Sunday school teacher in the church and he held a position as a deacon. I remember feeling so guilty inside, but I was falling so deep for Thomas that I just couldn't seem to stop myself. I never quite felt like I belonged anywhere, and at least I felt something besides pain and loneliness when I was with Thomas. I felt *wanted* and *needed*. I was blinded by my own desires and snared by the tricks of the enemy. We began seeing each other whenever we could. I would go out on late evenings to meet him at different places so we could spend time together. Looking back, I wish I wouldn't have done that, but I had chosen my path, and in doing so I was headed down a very slippery slope. We saw each other for a few months, and it didn't take long for us to get "busted". Thomas' wife had an idea something wasn't quite right. She finally put all of the pieces together and confronted him about it. Then, according to Thomas, she made him call my house one night while I was gone and together, they told my husband about what had been happening. I didn't get the privilege of telling my husband myself. But that's what happens when you choose to do the wrong kinds of things. Mitchell called me on my cell phone and said that he'd gotten a call from them, and that he'd told them that this better not be some kind of ploy to cause trouble. I believe Mitchell was in shock. I know he didn't want to believe it. I was the only woman he'd ever been faithful to, and he was completely blindsided by the whole thing. He never thought for one moment I'd do that, and to tell the truth, neither did I. I told Mitchell I'd talk to him when I got home. I was scared out of my mind, and I felt horrible inside. I went to a local park where there was a pond. It's a place I would often go to think. Sitting in my car, I wrote letters to Thomas, to my children, to Mitchell, to my mother, and to my brothers; and it was right there that I decided I did not want to live anymore. How could I ever live above what I had done? I was devastated. I felt that I was in love with Thomas, and I also felt humiliated at the same time, because he was going to stay with his wife and I knew it. Even if Thomas didn't stay with his wife, I knew God would never stand for this. He would never bless something that started with deception and sin. How would I ever explain all of this to my family? How would I respond to my children who would someday likely hear about their mother, the home-wrecker? How could I ever show my face in public? In the small town I lived in, everyone knew each other and scandals spread like wildfire. All I could think about is the fact that I felt that no one would miss me if I was gone; not even my kids, because in my mind, I'd be doing them a favor by "offing" myself. I mean, look at the person I'd become! They did not need a broken mess of a mother. At that moment, death seemed better than what I'd have to deal with alive. After writing the letters, my intention was to swallow a bunch of sleeping aids that I had from a prior prescription then put my car into gear and let it drive into the lake. I'd never know what hit me. No one would ever have to see my face again except to dispose of my body.

   I took the pills and got very sleepy. I opened my car door placed the letters on the ground in a plastic bag where I knew they would be found. I put the car in gear and let it roll forward. I got nervous and backed it back up. There was a really struggle going on in my head. I rolled the car down towards the water two more times and felt myself get extremely sleepy. In my head I could hear a voice saying, "Just do it! What are you waiting for? You need to be dead and you won't be a problem anymore", yet at the same time I could feel the pull of something or someone else reminding me that taking my life meant there was a possibility that I'd go straight to Hell; that I was taught better than this; that I needed to think of my kids; that my life wasn't over just because I'd messed up. It was a surreal feeling. The other voice was just as loud and it was all going on in my head at the same time. My emotions were all over the place from disappointment in myself, to anger, to shame and everything in between. Somehow, I still felt God's presence. Somehow, I still knew that even if no one else cared one bit about me, God loved me, but I just didn't feel that I could face all of that. I felt completely unworthy of God's love.

   I got very scared, backed the car back up, and put it in park. I still had a battle going on in my head for my life. I was so sleepy, I felt like I was going to pass out. I put the car back in drive, and I leaned over the wheel of the car, and I was so tired that I just couldn't fight it. It was "lights out" for me. The next thing I remember is waking up feeling like I'd been run over by a truck. Imagine my surprise that my car was *not* in the lake and I was not dead. I had every intention of dying that day. The car wasn't in drive. I didn't' understand why. When I slumped forward, somehow my purse had fallen in a way that had jammed the gearshift into park. At least that's how I figured it. I'm just not sure, but I guess God wasn't done with me yet. Good thing he wasn't, because I probably would have immediately entered the pits of Hell. My head hurt, and I felt sick; like I was going to puke my guts up. I don't know if I was in shock or what. I was also filled with so much fear and dread of what was to come that I called my cousin and asked her if I could come by to talk to her. I was crying my eyes out and she told me to come right over. I told her my story, and she told me never to do that again. She told me she loved me, and that people make bad decisions sometimes. She told me to think of my children. She told me that I could make it through this, and that she would be there for me. She prayed with me that night. I promised her I was going to go home and talk to Mitchell. She offered to go with me, because she was afraid of how Mitchell would respond, or that I may go back to the lake and finish it. I told her that I needed to go face the mess I made alone, and I went home.

Mitchell was anxious to see me. It must have seem like a million years to him for me to get home. I didn't even try to explain myself when he asked me if it was true. I began to cry, told him "Yes, it's true", and offered to leave the house. I fell on my face in the floor and began to sob. I had let my husband of eight years down. I had created a legacy I knew I'd never ever be able to erase. I felt like trash. I had ruined not only my life, but the lives of others, and I didn't know how I'd ever be able to live with that. I didn't know how I would ever face my children if they someday heard the truth. Most of all, I knew that God had to be disgusted with me. That hurt me so much inside, because God had never let me down. Mitchell told me to stay and that he needed some time to deal with it all, but that he wanted to try to work it out, so I stayed.

The days after that got harder and harder. I stepped down from my position as Sunday school teacher and asked the worship leader not to ask me to sing anymore. Thomas stepped down from his position as deacon. Everybody in the church knew what happened. Thomas' father was a preacher as well, and I know it was extremely hard for him and his family to have to look at me. That part hurt a lot, because I thought a lot of all of them. My family couldn't believe I'd done something like that. I still remember it as one of the hardest times of my life. I cannot express the lowliness I felt. I was close friends with Thomas' sister at the time, and I know it was very hard on her as well to watch it all unfold, yet she was one of the few that did not turn against me. I was recognized by many of the people I'd known at that church my whole life as a home-wrecker. I was shunned, and it angered and hurt me because I felt I had been pursued, but the problem with that is that after I got "hooked", in all honesty I think I called him as much as he called me. I wasn't the one to make the first calls or bring up feelings other than friendship, but I didn't resist participation in what I knew was wrong either. Hind sight is 20/20 and today I realize that doesn't matter, because I could have chosen not to fuel the fire. But I didn't; I went full-speed right into it. Wrong doing is wrong doing, and to shuck responsibility makes no sense whatsoever. It was just as much **my** fault or maybe even more.

I had heard a lot about what people were saying about me, and I couldn't see how I would ever be able to redeem myself as far as the church was concerned. After Thomas stepped down from his position as deacon, he had remained on stage playing his guitar during worship service. I was not about to get up there and continue my singing, unworthy as I felt and I doubt anyone there would have stood for it either. It was hard enough to take the looks, and most of the time after that (until I stopped going altogether) I kept my eyes on the floor to avoid any eye contact with anyone there, including the pastor.

Thomas and his wife began to seek counselling from the pastor and from another couple in the church. She started to come to church with him. It was hard for me to just let Thomas walk away. I felt more alone than ever. I loved him, and he'd told me he loved me too. I talked to him only a few more times after the whole thing blew up in our faces. I asked him why he was now acting like he didn't know me anymore, but I didn't get much of a response. It's actually better that way. But before I could get anywhere near "over him", the pastor of our church made a personal call to me and told me that if I "bothered Thomas again" that he would call me out on it in front of the whole church. I stopped going to the church that day. I was too humiliated, and too hurt. People there could barely look at me anyway; the same people that had taught me as a little girl, preached to me, and prayed over me. It sent a clear message to me that I was only "loved" conditionally. The pastor never offered me or my husband any assistance whatsoever. The only thing he had to say included threats instead of any kind of love or guidance. I felt I had nowhere to turn. I have never felt so alone, so desolate, so humiliated in every way. That pastor later ended up in divorce and was no longer pastoring a church anywhere; and last I heard he'd died. I felt sad, because I'd actually written him a letter at some point after the dust settled about the extra pain I felt he'd caused me by handling it the way he did, and I hoped it hadn't added to any stress for him if that was the case.

Thomas' wife ended up pregnant right around the same time this whole episode came to a head with a child they'd supposedly been trying to conceive for five years (according to him, because at that point he was aggravated at me for talking to him). I didn't understand how he could seem to be so acting so happy with his wife and so cold towards me after all he'd told me he'd felt for me. I felt like the biggest fool on the planet. It felt like I was nothing more than a fling. I was right back where I started on the inside, feeling like somehow life always managed to "go South" on me. I was so angry inside; angry that nobody ever seemed to just love me. It almost felt like everything was coming out sweet as a rose for Thomas, and I felt lower than I had ever been in my life. I gave up on the church I grew up in and I gave up on God too, whom I felt I had no right to even speak to or ask for forgiveness, because I'd broken a commandment; in fact, many of them. In my eyes, I was a lost cause, without redemption. I made more than one attempt to try to apologize to Thomas for my failure to do the right thing that led us down that rocky road. I apologized to his wife too at an alter one night. She said that she accepted my apology and that Mitchell and I needed to work things out, but her actions made me feel like what she was saying and what she really felt was two different things. I don't blame her, though. I would get to be on her side of the coin *multiple* times in the future. Apologies don't seem to feel like you've done enough to right a wrong that big anyway.

Anytime Thomas ran into me anywhere, he would look the other way and act like he didn't know me. So did she for the most part, or she made comments to antagonize me in front of him at public places that took me back to those same old feelings. I can't say I blame Thomas for avoiding me to keep peace at home, but I've often wondered what he's going to do if we both make it to Heaven, but I don't blame her for her feelings either. She was a victim, and it's much easier to lay the bulk of the blame on the person you *don't* love. It's something that I know I will never really be able to totally cast off (some things we do follow us forever), and it was all because of that split-second decision to take that "wrong" fork into that pitch-black path.

I know I can't live every day with regret. I know God has forgiven me and with his help I will be able to avoid making that same error again, but I also know that I will never forget the lessons I learned from it. I will never truly be able to shed it. Not as long as victims have to feel the pain from it. I did have to stop blaming Thomas for the whole thing and accept the fact that I played just as big a part as him and again, possibly even more. I was a little older than him, and I'd grown up in my church knowing better. At any time, I could have stopped participating in it, but I didn't. I became too fond of the feelings that I had around Thomas to want to do the right thing. I so desperately wanted someone to show they wanted me. As it progressed, I even called on him sometimes. So, I accept *my* responsibility in it all. It's something that I will live with until my time on this Earth is done, but I don't agonize over it anymore. Not like I used to, at least. It can still make me sad if I dwell on it long. I paid a costly price (not only me, but those attached to me as well). I finally "got" the lesson, and I can be grateful for what I learned through that situation. Thomas passed away later in life (younger than what we'd consider a timely death) due to an illness. I hate that part of his life was spent in duress thanks to *me* not choosing right for both of us. But I've forgiven him. It wasn't at any more fault than me, because I was in control of my own decisions. Unfortunately, I didn't learn soon enough that the problem was *me*. I had too much pain in my heart and too big a need to feel wanted and to "matter" and it made me make unwise decisions.

As for Mitchell and me, our marriage had taken a real beating. We decided to try to work out the marriage for the sake of our children. After a while things simmered down and for two years it was pretty quiet, as I tried to steady myself from the aftermath. You would think after watching the dominoes fall into disaster that I wouldn't choose another challenging path. But I guess I wasn't done learning yet. In fact, I was in for more pain down the same old roads. Like a broken record that kept playing the same old song, I kept having to learn the same old lessons.

Unfamiliar Territory

Now comes the biggest fork of them all; the story of the biggest decision I ever had to make in my entire life. It's the "fork" that would test me to the core. It's the journey that came with the most cost, and yet this path taught me the most valuable lessons that I've learned up to now, but it came with a very heavy price tag. Mitchell and I were still together two years after the affair.

During the time that the trouble really started brewing in the marriage, we'd joined the ranks of most Americans in the late 1990's and gotten a personal computer. It was actually a nice distraction for me. I felt very alone at that point and it was easier to live in a make-believe world. I was a stay-at-home Mom and I hadn't worked in several years due to the fact that we now had three young children, and the cost of day-care would have taken up 90% of whatever I could make at a full-time job. My three children were my life, but I rarely got to have adult interaction.

My husband worked a lot, and when he would come home, he would unwind by playing with the kids before retreating to the sofa to watch television until bedtime. We were still very disconnected emotionally, and I tried to talk to him about it many times. Mitchell didn't want to talk. I'm sure he felt as if he was being nagged all of the time, and who needs that? Conversations still usually ended with him saying he was tired and going to bed, and I would sit and cry alone feeling lonely as ever. I wanted him to see me, hear me, and be affectionate with me, or dance with me in the kitchen to a romantic song. I even tried that once and he started laughing about it and just stood there, so I just stopped and never attempted to get his attention like that again. He saw most of this as me being childish. Either way, the computer opened up a new world for me in the way of chat rooms. Nobody in chat rooms cared what I'd done, and they were *never* not there for me.

My third child had finally reached the age that he could start Kindergarten, and I wasn't in any rush to get back into the work force. I wanted to be able to pick them up after school. I wanted some time to myself, so I remained the typical housewife. I began to chat online with people and began to develop friendships with the people I met on the internet (I am still friends with a few of them today). In the internet world, I found people who were willing to do what my husband was not. They listened, offered words of encouragement, and even gave me a place where I could be something other than just a mother, housekeeper, or wife. I could be me. I forged friendships that gave me an escape from the real world and the fact that I had again become overweight, depressed, and lonely. I also felt like a bad mother. I'd always felt some sort of invisible wall between me and my children, or me and everyone in my life for that matter.

My boys were so independent; they didn't really seem to need me much and they were always super excited when their dad got home from work at the end of every day. I almost felt like they loved him more than me. That was my messed-up way of thinking. That came from never feeling good enough, or just flat unworthy of love. My own parents were never very affectionate. My mother's mother was not really close to her children either, and I'm not convinced that my mother really knew how to be very affectionate or play with us. I recall one time when I laid my head in my mother's lap and she played with my hair for a while. It's still one of my most heart-warming memories today. I admit I didn't really know how to be the mother I should have been to my three boys. My adoptive father (aka "my step-dad"); saw us in the very old-fashioned view of "Children are to be seen, but not heard" and he was a harsh, abusive man (my biological father was not in the picture until much later in life, as he left when he found out that my mother was pregnant and my step-father didn't want him in my life at all).

My "step-father" was abusive in every sense of the word. Just to give you a glimpse, we were told constantly as children that we would never amount to anything, that we'd be drug addicts, that we'd never have anything and that no one would ever really love us or stay with us. I was told that he made his peace with God before he died in 2005 from complications of lung disease (emphysema & COPD). Now that I'm older, I honestly believe that my mother and adoptive father did the best they could do with the tools they were given. I did the best I could do with the tools I was given.

Sometimes (well, more like all of the time) I wish I could go back and be more involved and affectionate with my own children, but you don't get "do-overs" in life. At the least I wish I'd had enough life skills to be the kind of parent that I needed to be with my boys. I kept them clean and fed, but what I wish I'd given them is more of my time. Beyond that, I didn't interact with them near as much as I should have, and that I will live with forever. You can't rewind the hands of time, so it's important to make every single day count with your loved ones. I believe it's very important to get help if you feel you are flailing around like a fish out of water when it comes to parenting. I sure wish I'd had a mentor. My parenting skills may have been better, or at least I'd had some guidance. Humiliation and feeling like a failure kept me from talking to anyone about what I was feeling inside. It was supposed to "come natural". It didn't and in that day and time, you couldn't say that out loud.

I made several friends in cyberspace. My internet friends afforded me companionship. They made me laugh. I began to feel somewhat alive again. I started to exercise a little and slowly began to drop a few pounds. I got excited about our meetings online. I paid less and less attention to my children or Mitchell.

Then, things started to get a little weird. There was a girl and a guy I typically hung out with in the chat rooms. The guy began to get a little possessive of me, spending a lot of time with me. I liked him. He was always there for me anytime I needed to talk, day or night. He knew that I wasn't really happy in my marriage. It felt safer to talk to someone "out there somewhere". He was such a great friend to me, offering words of comfort and reminding me that I was a wonderful person. In the meantime, I'd finally stopped trying to talk to Mitchell. Every time I would fuss about the things bothering me, he would say, "Whatever" or "You'll get over it!" Looking back, maybe after everything we'd been through, I have to wonder if he was just done with it all. I can't say I'd blame him. In his mind I was just "childish" or "immature". The truth is, I wasn't childish or mature. I was emotionally broken.

The very last conversation that I had with Mitchell, I told him that I wouldn't be coming to him anymore about anything and that I was tired of it beating my head against a brick wall. He told me again that I'd get over it, and for me that was it. That was the last time I ever wanted to hear those words. I gave up. I quit. Knowing Mitchell didn't really need me didn't do a thing for my insecurities or my feelings of being a "misfit", or that feeling that I didn't really belong anywhere I went, **ever**! It didn't help me feel like I mattered either. Emotional baggage can be crippling, and I was disabled by it for sure. I cannot blame Mitchell for the disconnection. I had not been able to truly connect with anyone most of my natural-born life despite attempts to win them over. Something was broken in me; terribly broken. Something was also broken in my marriage.

One Road Leads to Another

I'll never forget the day I asked Mitchell if he was ready to end it. He looked at me like I had three eyes, but he didn't argue about it or anything. He just said, "I'm not sure that's what's best for the kids, but if that's what you want, let's do it. Just tell me when." From there on, we drifted farther and farther apart. I remember scooting to the edge of our bed one night, thinking about what it really meant to be divorced; the finality of it, and asking myself if I really wanted to do it. I slid off of the bed with my mind made up, and my decision was to leave. If he didn't need me, I didn't need him. I'd taken my path in the "fork" in front of me and set the dominoes falling once again into the unknown.

After I slipped off the side of the bed that night, I walked to the spare bedroom. I stopped sleeping in the same room with Mitchell that very night, and I became more and more mesmerized by the only people that seemed to care about what I was feeling; my friends on the internet. Before I could get a handle on the marriage situation, something very odd happened. I'd been talking to my internet friends for almost a year. We regularly set chat dates, and one day my friend I'll call "Grant" came online earlier than usual. Grant would come online every day to talk to me. We'd "sit" beside each other in the chat rooms and entertain each other. He was witty, and always knew how to cheer me up. It was a big stress reliever. I could be someone besides just a mother that didn't seem to know what she was doing. I could distract myself from the fact that my husband still was not close to me, and that we were still just going through the motions. Mitchell and I were like roommates, and it made me sad. I was tired of trying to reach him. I cried many days and nights because of the helplessness I felt when it came to our marriage. I wasn't going to try anymore. All I could think of was how much he didn't seem to care.

Online, Grant kept me laughing and told me I was funny. He would tell me I was beautiful (I had a page on the internet that had a photo and he'd gone to the link to see what I looked like) and I began to develop confusing feelings for him; the same confusion that led me down the last path I took. Then one day it got more than just complicated. I was online when Grant came into the chat room and began talking to me. He didn't sound like himself. The phrasing was odd. The spelling changed, and something didn't seem quite right about it all. After chatting with him for a little while, I just outright confronted him and told him I had to wonder if he was really Grant.

He stumbled back and forth with his words until I got what I was waiting for; Grant really wasn't Grant after all. What I had been told all along was that Grant was married and going through a divorce, and that he had two daughters in the middle of it and was trying to save the marriage and sort it all out, but nothing was working. Now, I was being told by this person that "Grant" was actually a woman posing as a man online. Oliver, the soon to be ex-husband, was now logged in as Grant and he was looking for information. While it was true that they were married and going through a divorce, Oliver disclosed to me that he'd uncovered that his wife was posing as Grant online but pursuing a lesbian relationship with someone else that she was talking to online in a different chat room. Ironically, I'd met "Grant" in a religious chat room. I could not believe what I was hearing. I mean, I grew up in the middle of the Bible belt. People did not openly speak of homosexual relationships where I lived. But here it was in my face and I did not know what to do or say. Oliver wanted to see if "Grant" had ever disclosed any passwords to me for his personal email or given me any relationship details. Of course, I had none of that, because "Grant" had never disclosed his/her real identity. Even now, I was beginning to wonder "who was who" and which story was even the truth. Oliver asked me not to say anything so that he could continue to try to find out what was truly going on with his wife. My mind was reeling from information overload, shock, and disbelief. Once again, I had trusted the wrong person. Once again, I had been played a fool. Once again, my own decisions had taken me down into the pit of Hell.

 Later that evening, Grant came online again. Not knowing which person it was, I just waited for her to approach me. It was almost as if nothing had ever happened. Grant was just like "he" always was the many times we'd talked before, and I knew I was talking to the Grant that was a poser. Why would this woman do this to me? It didn't take long for it to get to me, and I confronted Grant. I told the story about how someone came online saying he was "the husband" and that Grant was not a man at all. I told Grant that Oliver came online trying to get information, and mostly I wanted to know why Grant would ever keep something like this from me. For crying out loud, I had shared my deepest secrets, fears, and worries! I'd begun to have questionable feelings for Grant, and now this?

 The answer I got was that she indeed was not Grant and was going through a very hard time with her marriage on the verge of ending, not to mention struggling with having lived a life as a heterosexual when she felt she was gay her whole life. She said she'd been trying to live the "normal" life for her family's sake, and that it just wasn't working anymore. She had met a woman online and had started somewhat of a relationship with her. She said that she'd wanted to tell me, but couldn't, because she cherished our friendship and was afraid, I would end the friendship if I knew she was really a woman. She didn't want to lose the only people that she felt were her friends. Believe it or not, I could relate to that. It's not like I was totally transparent online either. I must say this was a lot to take in and I was out of my mind by this point. To say I was in total shock would probably be an understatement. I wondered how in the world I found myself in the middle of this unbelievable drama. My whole life had been one big ball of drama. I am actually still friends with her today, though. She became a very faithful friend to me (even after marrying Oliver, her ex-husband) despite the circumstances that crossed our paths.

The days that followed were odd to say the least. Oliver got his own sign-on and would come online and talk to me to see how I was doing, and to talk about his anguish over what was going on in his life. I've always had a soft heart for hurting people and could relate as my marriage was all but dead as well. "Grant" pretty much faded away out of embarrassment and humiliation, I think.

Oliver seemed so genuinely hurt. I felt really bad for him. He was losing his wife to another woman which was the ultimate blow to a man, and he felt he would lose his kids in the process too. Oliver and I began to talk as friends trying to sort through a very strange situation. We confided in one another, we talked about our fears, and we commiserated about the way our lives were falling apart. We talked for months and thought it would be cool to hear each other's voices. We began talking on the phone from time to time. We began to be very fond of each other. It felt very good to have someone to lean on during a very scary time in my life. Before I knew it, I was falling for Oliver and the feeling was mutual. I looked forward to his calls every day or seeing him online. I was stuck in a marriage that had not really been a marriage in a very long time, and I just couldn't do it anymore. Things were so bad between Mitchell and me that he began hanging out with a friend and drinking with him occasionally and showing up late in the night which would lead to us fighting; fights that materialized in front of the kids. Mitchell probably thought I didn't care, because by that time I was online all of the time. The truth is, I did care and it hurt. It hurt badly, because it felt like Mitchell didn't even care enough about me to try to turn these things around. It seemed very odd to me that he had time for all of that, but I was not on his priority list. My childhood had some history with alcohol abuse, and any drinking at all sparked a fear in me that led to confrontations. He just grew more distant. I knew there was no use in trying to fix something that was never really right from the beginning, and I didn't want my kids to think "co-habitation" was normal in a marriage. I gave up at that point, because I had found comfort in someone else that Mitchell didn't seem to want to provide.

At one point, Oliver even flew out to see me and I met him in a nearby town. It felt SO good to have someone hug me, hold me, and care what I was feeling on the inside. Mitchell ended up finding some correspondence and letters between Oliver and I (even though he knew we would be seeing each other that weekend), and that pretty much put the final nails in the coffin of our marriage. He was very angry over it all, and so was I, because I felt that if he'd only listened to me and cared about me enough to be there for me and work with me on the marriage and go to church with me that it all could have turned out differently. He knew that we were divorcing, and had very little to do with me, so it made no sense to me that he was angry about it when he knew I was talking to Oliver. Mitchell didn't seem to want me anyway. If he did, I felt like

he would have changed his tactics after the last episode. I felt like I was never really important to him at all.
I was done pretending that everything was okay. We sat down one night and split up our marital community proper on paper and I filed for divorce from Mitchell in December of 1998 just a few weeks later. By February of 1999 the divorce was final. It was almost like some weird dream. We went to the courthouse and waited for our turn with the judge. Mitchell was even goofing with me making me laugh during the hearings. I guess he was trying to soften the blow. The judge final called us up and within minutes he pronounced us divorced. Believe it or not, we went to lunch after that and very little was said about what just happened. I was so numb I couldn't even cry. I don't know if it was a blessing or a curse. That decision was sending me down a very specific path whether I knew it or not, and unfortunately it would not impact just my life.

Starting Over in a New Place

Months after the divorce was final, Oliver invited me to Arizona to see him. His divorce had also been filed and was in the final stages. His wife had moved out with the two girls and now his belongings were in boxes and he was going to have to move in with his brother. He was a mess and he needed a friend. I had never been farther than Illinois, Alabama, or Georgia so to go out West was an adventure. I left the boys in the care of their father and went on a much needed "vacation".

Arizona was so much different from where I'd lived my whole life. It was mesmerizing! The scenery was different, the culture was different, and most of all I finally got a chance to spend time with someone who actually wanted to be close to me. I've never seen anyone cry as much as Oliver; especially a man. I was blown away by the fact that he was so kind and loving towards me and was sensitive enough to show his emotions. In my eyes he was every woman's dream. He understood what I was going through, because his marriage was ending too. We were both in a great deal of pain, and that made it very easy to relate to one another. Not to mention that I have never been able to stand seeing someone hurt, and I watched the man cry many times over the failure of the marriage or not being able to be with his children every day. I had to be there for him, and in return he was there for me. We were two kindred spirits also at the end of our ropes and clinging to each other.

While I was there, he talked to me about moving to Arizona. My concern was my children. He told me to come with or without my kids, that my kids would grow up some day and have their own lives anyway. He just wanted to be with me. At one point he got very upset when we were on a walk talking about whether or not I would come because I was having second thoughts, and I remember feeling terrible for him as I watched him hang his head and cry as he walked in front of me during our walk in the Arizona sunset. I thought about Oliver and I thought about my kids. I honestly believed that my kids would probably not miss me as much as Oliver would, because I didn't feel I was the greatest mother in the world and they seemed just fine with me gone, or just being with their dad. To me it seemed, much like their dad, that they were perfectly okay with or without me around. Why wouldn't they though? I wasn't exactly a prize- winning mother. In my mind, I was still telling myself that I could bring them back to the desert with me and the rest would work out. I stayed a few weeks and it was awful when I had to leave. Oliver and I were both very emotional and we didn't want to let each other go. I believe it is because we were going through some of the same things and we naturally just clung to each other. At any rate, I had decisions to make and it was time to go home. Needless to say, it was a very emotional goodbye.

Once I got home and Mitchell asked me how I liked it in Arizona. I told him I really did like it and could see myself living there. He wasn't fond of the idea of his kids being that far away, but he was willing to let me take them with me with the understanding that we'd have joint custody of them and that he could see them whenever he wanted, and also get them for summers. Oliver and I missed each other so much after I left Phoenix. We stayed in touch by phone and we did everything we could do to figure out how we could be together. Oliver lived with his brother for a while then finally bought a house of his own. Once his divorce was final, he'd said he wanted to be a family and he couldn't wait to get me there. He asked me to come to Arizona to get set up and with a very heavy heart, I left my boys in the temporary care of my mother and went out

West to try to stabilize myself again before bringing them back to the desert. Mitchell had loaded up a truck with my portion of the "household community property" and took me halfway to meet Oliver. I'm not sure now if I was running from the pain of a broken first marriage, or if I was just running to anyone to avoid being alone. At any rate, I knew I loved Oliver and I desperately needed to feel like someone really loved me. He'd pulled me out of a very dark place emotionally, and I wanted to be with him.

    Mitchell asked me the night before I left if I was sure I wanted to really do this, and I told him I wanted to go. The whole time I was sobbing. It hurt so bad to know I'd be away from my kids, but it hurt bad being with someone that wasn't really into me too. To tell the truth, on the inside I was so unsure about what I was doing that it wasn't funny. I was excited and scared to death at the same time. The night before I left, I slid to the edge of the bed and asked myself, "What if Oliver is not who I think he is? What if I am doing the wrong thing?" I dismissed it and got my clothes together for the next day. I was living with Mitchell in the same house, but he felt like a stranger to me. I wanted to be "home". That's all I'd ever wanted; to feel like I belonged **somewhere**. Anywhere!

The Temporary U-Turn

Once I got to Arizona, I almost felt like I was in a dream. My heart was hurting because I had to leave my children behind. I loved Oliver so much, but I loved my boys too. I kept replaying the conversation in my head to my boys, telling them we were all going to be okay and that I had to go to Arizona and set up a place for us and that it would seem like I was going to be gone for a long time, but I'd come back for them. My oldest son was crying when my mother had picked them up to take them to her house the night before Mitchell was to take me to meet Oliver in Texas. He was trying to hold it back, but I saw the pain. That was the hardest thing I've ever done. I really believed it was only a matter of me getting everything set up, getting my boys to Arizona, and life would be good. To this day, I cannot believe my thinking was so clouded. What I do remember is that I really felt that getting away from a place that had been so full of failure and pain was the smartest thing to do. I thought it would allow me to start over with a clean slate, and that all I needed to do was get myself there.

I will insert here that no matter where you go in life, you take yourself with you. So again, I say, "wherever you go, *there you are!*" You can get away from places, but you can't get away from yourself. I could have run to the farthest end of the Earth, and I still wouldn't have been able to get away from the pain that had gripped my heart; a *lifetime* of pain.

Oliver was forever talking about how we would finally have the "good life" together and all I needed to do is get to Arizona. Once I got there, it really started to bother me that we were living in the same house as a couple. My convictions were getting the best of me. I was there a few months when I asked Oliver when we were getting married. I had told him plenty of times that I would not just live with him. It was against my moral convictions. I know this sounds crazy considering I'd seen him before my divorce was completely final and considering my past shortcomings, but it was something that really got to me. He'd said we were going to get married when I got to Arizona. I had the whole house set up, waiting for my children and I couldn't wait to go get them. Oliver assured me we would get married before long, but I was there almost 6 months and we still weren't married and I knew then that he was stalling. He wanted me to go get my kids and wait a while, and that he could be committed to me "without a piece of paper", but I felt it was just another rejection from yet another man I'd given my heart to, and after several discussions where I ended up crying my eyes out, and feeling deceived, I packed up my things and asked my brother and Mitchell to come get me.

Even as I waited for them to get there, I wasn't sure I wanted to go. As it turned out, they came and I got scared at the last minute and they ended up taking my things back to Tennessee. They left me there to figure out what I really wanted to do. Oliver was heartbroken and emotional, asking me not to leave. Mitchell was frustrated that he'd come all that way just for me to flake at the last minute. I think he did feel bad for making me feel bad for calling him for help though, because he told me to really think on things. Just in case things didn't go well, my things were going back home with Mitchell and my brother.

I stayed with Oliver in Arizona and waited another two or three months before finally giving him an ultimatum. I was not about to "shack up" in front of my children. I told him that we either got married, or I was going back to Tennessee and we'd have to try to figure it out from a distance, or maybe even just forget the whole thing. He didn't seem willing to hold up his end of the agreement, so I loaded my clothes in the car and went back home. My heart was breaking the whole way, and my trust was broken as well. I didn't get it. My biological father had left me at birth, my first husband couldn't seem to connect with me in ten years, I'd ended up being nothing more to Thomas than a mistress, and now Oliver was getting wishy-washy on me too. I felt like my heart would explode from the pain.

Oliver and I didn't speak for a while after that. I was beside myself. I missed Oliver really bad, but I was not about to call him with my tail between my legs. I ended up renting a little shack for me and my boys, and I didn't even have a job. My car was a "junker". I had no idea how in the world I was going to make it. I have to say, I was hurting so bad inside that I almost couldn't breathe. I'd been through so much in the past few years and now I found myself alone with my boys, not knowing how in the world I'd take care of them. I hadn't worked in two or three years, because I'd been a stay-at-home mom. I was trying to make ends meet on the child support Mitchell was paying me, look for a job, and get three kids to school every day all alone, and I was so scared. I was an emotional basket case. I wondered if the divorce from Mitchell had been the right thing to do. I was hurting because I truly had fallen for Oliver and I couldn't believe he'd do this to me after I went all the way to Arizona to be with him. I was questioning if I'd ever be able to take care of my kids by myself and I felt like a miserable, rejected mess.

At one point, I asked Mitchell if we could try one more time to put things back together. He told me that I was just scared to be alone and that he would have to "think about it". I knew in my heart that he would not be back, so it really chalked up to another rejection for me; a confirmation to me that he never really cared for me in the first place. To tell the truth, maybe he was right. Maybe I **was** just scared. I was also confused in the worst way. Why did it seem like every single person in my life could not seem to just love me? In the meantime, Oliver said he was missing me. He would call and cry and tell me that he was sorry and that if I'd just come back, we could get married and live happily ever after. I was not about to fall for that again, so I told him I would never move back there again to live with him and be deceived again. We had arguments about it on the phone and at one point he totally avoided me for two entire days, and wouldn't answer my calls or anything.

    I remember crying myself to sleep that night, wondering why I couldn't seem to mean something to the men in my life. I was so messed up at that time in my mind and so scared that I couldn't even see straight. I cried and cried and my oldest son, only eight years old at the time, came to check on me and rubbed my back. My precious boy told me he loved me and was sorry I was sad. I will never forget that moment. That young boy was more of a man in my eyes at that moment than any of the men that had ever been in my life. Yet my choices after that would damage even that relationship, a regret that is with me to this day even after we've been slowly working through it for years. I will never get over how I allowed anything to put distance between me and my babies, and I don't understand it to this day, but the devil is a sly, old snake.

    I started having bouts of anxiety melt downs. I wasn't handling any of it well. Once I even had to call Mitchell to come sit with the boys because I was having a mini breakdown and I didn't want them to see it. I cried and cried, agonizing over the mess my life was becoming. He sat with our children and told me I needed to get a grip of myself; and that I'd be fine. To me it was the same old story. "You'll get over it. You'll be fine. Your feelings don't matter." Why could no one seem to see that I was dying inside? That I'd always been dying inside? Why couldn't anyone really **see** me? I kept calling Oliver, because he was the only one that I seemed to be able to connect with at all. I needed desperately for someone to want me, and he felt like my only option. He kept not answering the phone. I was the biggest, broken mess and I wasn't seeing the truth right in front of me!

On the Road Again

Oliver must have had a change of heart, because he finally answered my call one day and told me he was sorry. I wondered how I could ever place my faith in him after the way he'd avoided me and left me feeling abandoned. How could he have known what I was feeling and just not talk to me? I should have paid attention to the red flag that waved right in my face, but I dismissed it as Oliver being incredibly stressed having been through a divorce, adjusting to having his children only every other weekend, and being away from me. He was doing his best to make it up to me, and I bought it hook, line, and sinker. I convinced myself that somehow his behavior was entirely my fault.

It was a very nerve-wracking couple of months of us going back and forth before I finally told him I'd come back, but the catch was we had to be married before I would go. Call it insanity, but I was about to be met head-on with yet another fork-in-the-road, and I was about to send the dominoes flying again as if I hadn't learned a **thing**! After stalling another month or so and arguing back and forth, Oliver decided he couldn't live without me and ended up flying to Tennessee in September of 1999 and we were married by the Justice of the Peace. One more time I had to leave my children behind with Mitchell to get myself settled in Arizona. But this time, I was convinced it would be different. I arrived in Phoenix, my final destination and began sending out resumes to local jobs nearby. I somehow fooled myself into believing I was going to have the "perfect life" with Oliver, my kids, a white picket fence, and a dog.

Times were very hard for me during those times. I was crazy about Oliver, but I missed my children so bad I couldn't sleep at night. I talked to them at least every other day, but it wasn't like seeing them. My heart was breaking. I would get very emotional quite frequently, and had it not been for my step-daughters I don't know what I'd done. They gave me something to hold onto while I was waiting to get my boys. Finally, it seemed everything was finding some order, and I went back to Tennessee to pick up the boys and bring them back to what would finally be our home together. I stayed there for a few weeks, and things got a little tense again between Oliver and me. He seemed moody, and he told me if I was coming back home I needed to come now. He was tired of waiting. I was afraid that I was losing him, and I decided I'd better get back. After borrowing some cash to get back to Arizona (Yes, I had to do it myself and that should have been a sign). I met Mitchell near his work to tell the boys a quick "Goodbye" before we left. It hurt my heart to see him staring after us after I pulled onto the highway with our boys in tow, but I was glad I finally had my children with me and I headed west.

   I was thinking Oliver would be waiting for us at home when we made that twenty-two-hour trip, but when we got there Oliver had gone to play volleyball as normal. That struck me as odd, because I thought he'd said he missed me and couldn't wait to see me. Then, where was he?!?!?! I had to find a hidden key just to get into the house. Once the boys and I got in and had a moment to rest, I began putting our things away. We really didn't have much, so within a few hours it all had a place. Oliver finally got home and I ran to greet him and get the boys more acquainted. I was so excited to be in his arms again. He seemed to feel a little out of sorts or awkward which sent off an alarm in my head, but I quickly dismissed it as part of the big changes we were going through until he said, "Wow, you wasted no time." I asked him what he was talking about, and he pointed to the empty boxes. I told him we really didn't have much and he didn't respond, but something about it didn't feel right. It seemed to be a problem that I'd just come right in and put our things away, but I was just so happy to be with him again that I didn't want to think about it so I let it go. It was going to be a new experience for us all, and I knew that. We began the adjustments of being a blended family. After all, the good life was just beginning.

Feeling Like a Foreigner

Sometimes things don't work out like you planned. Things felt very odd in the house. Oliver acted like he wasn't quite sure how to relate to the boys and in turn, they acted as though they were equally uncomfortable. It was unnerving for me, but I figured with time we would all adjust. Over time, it only got worse. The boys really missed "home" and the youngest finally asked me one day when we were moving back to Tennessee. I tried to explain to him that I was married now and this was supposed to be our new home. Over the next couple of months, they still seemed somewhat miserable and sad. They were not adjusting like I'd hoped.

To add to that, Oliver and I had a few arguments here and there because he was a little "flirtier" with his female friends than was acceptable to me. I'd found some porn on his computer too, and he'd assured me that he'd had it on there before we were married. Now that I was here with him, he explained, he wouldn't need it anymore. This infuriated me because it was one of the things I talked to him about right off the bat. I'd had some issues with porn and my first husband. I didn't like it. It made me feel uncomfortable, and I didn't want to go through it again. I was uncomfortable with it because of a few things, one of them being the fact that my step-father had taken us to see a pornographic movie at the drive-in with my mother once and it left me feeling very disturbed. It left my mother feeling disturbed too. At any rate, Oliver had assured me I had nothing to worry about because he wasn't into it, so when I found it on his computer by accident one day, it hit me like a ton of bricks. There was tension in the house and it only added to the boys wanting to go back east to Tennessee.

Finally, with a broken heart, I told the boys if they really wanted to go back home, I would let them. I was at another crossroads and it was one of the hardest decisions I've ever had to make. I had never had the option of getting to know my biological father, much less an option to be with him. I didn't even meet him until I was fifteen years old and my mother had to sneak around to make that happen. When my adoptive father found out about it, it caused a holy war in the house. He'd married my mother when I was about eighteen months old and, in his eyes, I was his property. I was not to even mention my biological father. I held a lot of resentment inside for years, especially for the way he treated us. I did not want my kids to ever feel like they did not have a choice. I didn't want them to go back to Tennessee, but I figured if I didn't let them, they might grow up resenting me because I held them back. I also realized they might end up feeling that I didn't care about them because I let them go. I decided I'd rather take the chance on giving them their own choice, even if it meant I had to be the one to lose. Mitchell had always been a good father, and I knew he would do a wonderful job with them. If they wanted to go back, who was I to keep them?

The dynamics in Oliver's house made all of us feel a little uncomfortable, and I did not want my boys to be uncomfortable in their own home. God knows I'd felt like an outsider my whole life. My family didn't understand any of this at all and many of them saw me as a mother that abandoned her children because I let them go without me. After my children left, it took me a long time to cope. Thank God Oliver's girls came over every other weekend. It was the only thing that kept me sane. I still missed my boys with everything in me, but having the girls around made it easier to bear. I went through months of crying spells, not sleeping, and having meltdowns. Oliver was very understanding, and he tried to offer comfort and distract me whenever he saw me in pain. I knew I would only see my boys on holidays and during summer visits and it was devastating to me, but I wanted them to be happy more than anything else. Summers would prove to be just as hard as our initial experiences in Oliver's house. It never did get better.

With my boys now in their father's care, I began my job search. It took a few months, but I finally found a job. I started out as a receptionist for a flight school. It made my days easier, because I wasn't just sitting around the house with every minute ticking by so slowly, thinking about how far away I was from my children. For a while things were good, but I can't say they were great. Oliver was still playing volleyball, and sometimes he'd ask me if I wanted to go but I didn't really appreciate it all that much because I'd have to watch him playing around with his lady friends in a way that made me flat uncomfortable, and something didn't seem right about it.

Oliver's whole personality changed around women. He had a female friend that would call him from time to time too which wouldn't have been a big deal had it not been for me hearing the way she talked to him, and one morning she called him at 6 o'clock am asking him to talk to her and I could hear part of the conversation. I asked him that morning why any woman would call her married male friend that early in the morning and that I didn't appreciate hearing her talk in a rather seductive voice to him. It ended up in a blow-up on the weekend when his girls were there. The same woman called again about a month later looking for Oliver, and I tried to politely set her straight and let her know I didn't appreciate her early morning calls or the way she talked to my husband. Friends were okay, but the relationship between them made me nervous, and Oliver's ex-wife had told me that this same woman had caused problems in their marriage prior to their divorce. This friend of his acted like she had no idea we were married. She said she thought he was "divorced". I let her know that he was, but he was also remarried. She told me he was a grown man and could do what he wanted which ignited my temper. I let her know that he was a grown man, with a grown wife that didn't appreciate a woman calling her husband all of the time, and especially in the wee hours of the morning in a seductive tone. Oliver was furious. He turned it all around on me, saying I was controlling and insecure and that he wasn't allowed to have friends. It only fueled the fire that began to burn in our marriage.

    I kept finding pornography on Oliver's computer which he swore he wasn't doing anymore, and that set the tone for years to come. I called them "cycles". I'd catch him doing porn online again, signing up for dating services, or in a lie which led to a confrontation. He was very good at silent treatment. Sometimes he would not look at, talk to, or even acknowledge me and this could last anywhere from a few days to months at a time. He was an absolute pro at the silent treatment. It was very hard for me. Here I was far away from all of my friends and family and Oliver, the only one I had in Phoenix, would just pretend I didn't exist. It made missing my boys even harder. I had to wonder what in the world was going on. This man who'd loved me so much he flew to Tennessee to marry me and bring me back was not the person I thought he would be, and I was taken back to the memory of that night I sat on the edge of the bed wondering if I should really divorce Mitchell, asking myself if Oliver was the man I thought he was and also asking myself, "What if he isn't? What then?" I'd dismissed my fears because Oliver was so very loving to me, and because he had impressed me so with his attentiveness, his sweet personality, and mostly his sensitivity to my emotions. I didn't think he would ever let me down. Now, here I was, feeling like I was on a road to a place that might not be a good place to be, and I was scared.

Caught Up in Madness

More and more Oliver and I began to argue, mostly about his porn habit. He could not go more than two days without spending five to six hours a day on porn. I cannot explain how inadequate it made me feel. He was looking at things that horrified me. It was very hard-core stuff and the more he looked at the more he wanted to look at it. It wasn't just a picture here or there. It was like an addiction. He was a courier for an engineering firm and his job was to deliver blue prints to other companies all day long. His boss had no clue when he was actually working or how long those deliveries took so he would go home during his "lunch break" every day and stay on the internet on porn for hours. They were clueless. Sometimes he would check out dating sites, or call dating phone lines. It angered me and I brought it to his attention all the time that not only was he disrespecting me, but he was using time his company was paying for to do it. Nothing was more important to Oliver than his habit.

The fights progressively got worse and Oliver started to show more and more aggression. Sometimes he would kick walls or furniture in anger if confronted or questioned about things. Of course, he always maintained that he wasn't doing anything. He also told me that the only reason we fought is because I wouldn't just leave him alone. He did what he wanted with whom he wanted, but I couldn't have friends. I felt very isolated. Even female friends would stoke him to lay guilt trips on me about being needy and he would tell me I was needy and weak and then talk about the fact that he didn't need friends or have friends. I couldn't even go to church without a guilt trip ensuing. Meanwhile, Oliver was off doing whatever he wanted with no regard to what it was doing to our marriage. I finally stopped talking to any friends that called when he was there, because it was just easier. I could avoid the guilt trips and fights. Something felt very wrong inside. Things kept getting worse and worse. Sometimes the arguments would get so intense I'd sleep on blankets in the garage because I felt so unworthy to be near him and he made it very clear to me that we were living in "his" house. At times he would not look at me, nor would he answer if I uttered a word to him. This would go for weeks to months at a time. I would pray and cry myself to sleep. I would beg God to help me change in a way that Oliver would not do these things anymore. I begged God to save my marriage.

People often ask me, "What kept you there if he was doing all of those things?" Well, just as quickly as the madness began it would end. Once Oliver was through his "mad spell", he would become the most loving man you ever met in your life. He would take me to dinner, to see a movie, or sometimes on a trip to a place I'd never been. He would become the doting husband. He'd buy me gifts. He'd romance me and make me laugh. He would tell me how much I meant to him and apologize for doing anything that caused me pain or stress. He'd tell me he was only testing me to see if I was spying on him, and that he really wasn't doing all of those things because he needed to do it. He would say I had pushed him to do those things. When he was good, he was very good. When he showed love, he would shower me with it. During those times I would question myself as to why I started the fights. The man had me so confused in my head that I even questioned myself as to what the big deal was, and why I made him "try me" like that. He had a way of making me feel that whatever issues we had, were all my doing. He reminded me that I had been "damaged" by my childhood and previous marriage and he would say he couldn't let me damage him too. He'd always follow up with crying, making himself appear the victim. I would feel horrible for making my husband feel anything bad. He made me feel that I had become an abuser. Looking back, I see that I was being brain-washed to feel guilty for doing anything that interfered with his addictions. But hind sight is 20/20. While you are in the midst of it, you are not sure what to feel. So, you begin to believe in what the ones you love and trust are telling you. We went through these cycles for years.

My boys would come for summers and it would always lead to drama. I never knew when Oliver would switch moods on me. He could get mad for the simplest reasons: leaving a light on, forgetting to close a cabinet, saying the wrong thing, or just about anything. It almost felt sometimes like he looked for reasons to be angry at me or irritated by something the boys did or didn't do. It got so bad that I started stressing about when my kids would come for the summer because he made us all feel so uncomfortable, and I didn't want our visit to be like that. I could tell that sometimes the boys weren't sure what to do and they'd just hide out in the bedroom. I can't say I blame them. I could see the odd look in their eyes that made them feel out of place. I wish I had a dollar for every time I feel asleep crying, feeling so guilty for what I was putting my kids through and not knowing how to fix it.

Oliver would also go through cycles when he would sleep in the other room for weeks or even months at a time, or I would because he would make it very clear he wanted nothing to do with me. This included intimately. It was like I was living in a stranger's house at times. Sometimes he would rage when we would get into arguments. He would tell me that I made his blood boil, and that he was afraid he might hurt me some day. The look in his eyes would send chills down my spine. I didn't know him anymore. I tried to talk to him. I did not want to go through another divorce. I had come to Arizona to make a new life, and to leave all of the drama and pain from my past behind me. How could it be that things could be like this?

    I prayed so hard for God to fix me, our marriage, or Oliver. I had letters upon letters of him expressing his love to me in the beginning, saying he wanted to marry me, and all of those types of things. How could he say things like he never wanted to be married to me? I tried to remind him of how much we loved each other. I tried to help him understand how important family was because I'd learned that lesson the hard way. I thought he'd learned the lesson too. I was hurting so bad. He was up one day, down another. One day he was the doting husband, and the next he wouldn't even acknowledge me in a room. He'd purposely not speak to me while he laughed on the phone and talked to his family, girls, or friends. He'd operate completely different with everyone else but me. It hurt me to my very soul. I'd trusted this man to love me and take care of my heart. I'd left everything I ever knew behind, and this was not going the way I planned. I couldn't bring myself to talk to my friends or family back home about it much because I didn't want to hear, "I told you so". I also didn't want them to worry about me. I'd only confided in a couple of friends when I finally just stopped, because I kept choosing to stay in the middle of the chaos so I knew they were probably tired of hearing it. Plus, I felt stupid and stuck at the same time.

The Road to Discovery

    For a while I'd been playing recreational volleyball with Oliver and his friend on Mondays, and sometimes practice games on weekends. One night, Oliver kept asking me if I was going to play or not. That was odd to me. I'd always gone and he'd never questioned me like that, but I did express that I might take a break that night. He'd just never acted that way, and it felt like he was up to something. At one point, someone called him on his cell phone and he was leaned over the counter talking in a shallow, muffled voice as if he was trying to hide something. I heard him tell someone he was "going to play" and asked them if they were going. When I asked him who he was talking to, he told me that his friend from one of the companies he delivered to and her husband were going. Something smelled fishy about the whole thing. Every time he'd ever lied to me, he got a certain look on his face. He was a habitual liar, but not a good one. I knew he was not being truthful. I waited until he left and had been gone a while then I drove over to the park where he was supposed to be practicing. It was dark so it wasn't hard for me to park in the shadows and just watch. I did see a girl there, but no husband. She was the young blond he'd helped to get a job as the receptionist where he worked. She was getting into his truck. They left together and I went home. My heart sank inside my chest. I don't know why I didn't follow them further, except that I felt like the breath had been knocked right out of me. I didn't say a word to him about it for several days. When I finally brought it up, he was furious. He told me that nothing had happened between them, and that she had injured her knee during practice and he had to take her to the hospital so she would not be alone. That hurt me deeply, because I'd been hospitalized at least twice where I was actually put to sleep and he'd dropped me off at the emergency or same day surgery door. He had never stayed with me. He'd always tell me I was going to be fine. How could he feel this kind of compassion for her, and the person he'd been married to for seven years or more he could just abandon when I needed him the most? When I asked him why he lied about her having a husband, he said that he knew if he'd told the truth that I'd swear he had something going on with her; that my jealousy was the reason we always ended up in these fights. The house was very, very quiet for a while after that. He wouldn't talk to me at all. When things did get somewhat normal, I felt very bad about it. I had to wonder if he was telling the truth, and if I'd made him feel bad just for having a friend. I knew how that felt and I didn't want to be that person. Our anniversary was approaching and I set up a mini trip a few hours away with the intent of making things better and getting back to our roots and the way we felt in the beginning.

The anniversary trip was rather strange. At first, we felt awkward and both of us were rather quiet, but it ended up turning out to be a halfway decent trip. He warmed up to me in a day or two and I was hopeful that things would turn around for us. Remember: even during the fighting and madness when he was good to me, he was very good to me. He could be the most loving person ever. That's what kept me hopeful that we could work things out. I would see one glimpse of "good" in him and I would hang onto that during the times he rejected me. I loved Oliver with all of my heart, and I wanted so badly for our marriage to work. I just couldn't shake the feeling that something was very wrong. My spirit was stirring. They say a woman just has certain intuitions. I sure could have used the experience that Thomas' wife had those years before, but there is no way in the world I would have turned to her. I was about to see how it felt to be on the receiving end of that kind of pain.

I felt something coming and I didn't feel like it was going to be good. The fights slowed. Things seemed to be looking up, but I have to admit that my heart was still on guard. Oliver even invited me to his work one day, and I went to his pine derby race. He'd made his own little "car" and he was pretty excited about racing it. I got there and the same blond receptionist, Jena, was there. I'd never said anything to her about the whole volleyball incident, though I'm sure he did. I introduced myself as Oliver's wife and asked if he was available. Jena pointed me down the hall, but I couldn't help but notice she seemed very unnerved by my presence. She was a cute girl, and about half Oliver's age (and younger than me) and I noticed that she wasn't in the same physical shape I was in either. I'd lost a ton of weight during the trying times of our marriage trying to get my husband's attention. I worked out all of the time, and I was looking better than ever. I breathed a little sigh of relief. Surely, he wouldn't do that to me.

Maybe he really had lied about her having a husband because he didn't want me to flip out for no reason. I wish that confidence had lasted, but Oliver who had been very loving and touchy-feely with me seemed a little different in Jena's presence. It was very odd, and I was already on high alert with her reaction when I'd arrived. Oliver stayed on the other side of the room after the race was over, and until one of the guys he worked with asked him if he was going to get his wife a plate, he barely acknowledged me at all. The receptionist, Jena, was there too and she wouldn't even make eye contact. She was very nervous. At one point I saw him lean over and say something to her, but I figured it was work related, because not long after that he came and stood by my side and had his hand on my hip. After the races, I pecked him on the cheek and went off to shop some until he got off work, oblivious to the truth.

As more time passed, I noticed Oliver was getting back into his same old moods again. He was avoiding me more and more and it seem like every little thing seemed to set him off. I was very frustrated, because it seemed we'd just gotten through a lot of trying experiences and now it appeared the storm wasn't over. The same tense air filled the house. Oliver would barely talk to me some days, then some days he'd be the funny, loving guy I had fallen in love with in the first place. It was almost like a repetitious cycle he'd go through every couple of months.

At one point he'd brought some pictures home from a work function and Jena, the receptionist, was standing next to him in the picture. Oliver had his arm around her. I was still uneasy about him being around her because of the lie he'd told when she met him at the volleyball park that night. In my mind, if she was only a friend, he'd never lied about her in the first place. I never saw pictures of him and any guys he knew from work or the places he delivered. I asked him why all of these females seem to need to be stuck to his hip all of the time, and he got very angry. He accused me of having serious self-esteem issues and attacking him for no good reason. He told me I was being abusive to him like "those people" in my childhood and that he was not going to let me abuse him too anymore.

Things got really rough that night. He yelled, he screamed, and he got in my face several times telling me I'd gone mad. He told me I was controlling. He told me something was "wrong with me in my head". He said a lot of things that made me feel like my heart had been turned inside out. I spent that night crying in my usual place in the garage on blankets, asking God like so many times before what I needed to do to fix me, and to fix our marriage. I took a risk and talked to one of my best friends that night in the dark in my garage, and she cried with me and told me I really needed to think about whether this relationship was good for me or not. She told me I was worth more than this. She also told me that she was scared for me. Oliver must have been eaves-dropping, because he took the opportunity now that he was angry at me to give me more silent treatment. He slept in the other room for four months. Yet, he would answer calls on his cell phone from others and go outside to take the calls. I could hear him laughing and carrying on and I knew he absolutely didn't care about what he was doing to me. I didn't know what to do anymore. I knew something was going on and he wasn't going to tell me. If I wanted to know, I'd have to find it all out on my own. It was then that I decided I needed to know for sure if something was going on behind my back, and desperate times call for desperate measures, they say.

    The next day I installed a key logger on our home computer. The key logger would take snapshots of every page looked at on the computer at home every couple of minutes. In addition, it would keep a record of every keystroke keyed-in on the computer and save passwords to things like emails. It also saved a list of all websites accessed and would email all of the collected information to the email address of your choice. I also installed it on my work computer despite the risk of being caught, just so I could remotely look at what Oliver was doing in real time. I have to say; my heart sank the first time I logged in and saw him online. I was hoping I would be wrong. I was hoping I'd find out that he was being truthfully with me, and my insecurity was the whole problem. I don't know why shock hit me like a ton of bricks that day. I knew in my heart he was still looking at pornography even though he said he wasn't. But to see it in real time, page by page, and what he was doing with it was very hard for me. I got way more than I expected, and sometimes the truth can be crushing. He was looking at a lot of hard-core porn of women in very compromising positions, and some of them looked very young and under-developed. It was disturbing and it hurt. I ended up having to see a doctor and get anti-depressants, because I literally felt like I was on the verge of a nervous breakdown. I felt like I was losing it. I was dealing with a lot of pain, and I had no idea how to handle it. I didn't tell Oliver that I had the key logger or what I'd seen, because as much as it hurt, I wanted to see more. I needed to know how bad it was, and the only way to do that was to gain more information. Not only was he visiting tons of porn sites every day, but he was saving pictures, zooming into them, and even manipulating them.

I knew of one of the ladies, Gayle. Oliver knew her for years. She was an office manager at a company that he delivered blueprints to for his workplace, and she was married but it didn't stop him from meeting her for lunch behind my back or sending her emails flirting with her. Gayle and I had a few conversations about my issues with Oliver and she told me to stop hounding him and that I was driving him away by being so jealous, and I started to actually doubt myself. Gayle was beautiful. She was Oliver's age or maybe a little older, but could it be that I was over-reacting? Oliver had told me many times that they were not friends, and that Gayle was just someone he knew from delivering there for so many years. But she made it sound like they'd been friends forever. He made me feel so bad for my insecurities about their friendship. Imagine how I felt that day when I saw him via the key logger actually manipulating a pornographic picture by cropping faces of these women that he knew on them! He'd taken pictures of receptionists and office managers where he made his deliveries, and now he was making his own pornography of people he knew such as Gayle. Some of the women I recognized and some I didn't. I felt sick inside, but I had to keep going. The key logger captured Oliver's passwords too, and I knew that it was wrong to spy but I wasn't going to get the truth from Oliver and if something was going on I didn't want to be the last one to know. A part of me didn't want to face the truth, but I reluctantly went into his email and started reading the messages in his inbox. Each one ripped open the wound in my heart bigger and bigger and made me feel like a complete fool.

No Denying the Truth

There are no words to describe what I felt the moment I saw the truth before my very eyes. Even though I halfway expected it, I almost felt as if someone had physically hit me with blunt force. My head hurt, and my heart started palpitating. There was a ringing in my ears and a sick feeling in my stomach. I literally felt like I was going to pass out. I had to close my eyes for a moment. The room felt like it was spinning. I couldn't even cry. There it was in black and white: emails between Oliver and Jena, the receptionist at his work. There were graphic emails discussing what he wanted to do to her, how excited she made him sexually, how he wanted to meet her somewhere, and how he needed to come up with a way to "disappear on someone" from the house to do that. He told her how sexy she was, and all I wanted to do is crawl under a rock and die. He hadn't called me those things in a long time. He had denied me emotional and intimate attention so many times and here he was lavishing it freely upon someone else.

He even talked about hiking with her in the moonlight. That's something he'd told me he wanted to do with me many times, but we had never actually done it. It stung my heart to the core. Jena responded with the same kind of excitement that I had years before she ever knew him. Oliver also had emails to Gayle telling her she was beautiful and asking if she ever thought of him, and about meeting for lunch again. He'd told me he'd never seen her outside of work. It made me highly suspicious about her acting like they were just friends too. I already knew that she and her husband had some problems in the past as well. I didn't trust anyone at that point. I printed all of the emails, the manipulated pictures, websites, passwords and everything I could find before I had to leave work. I was already late getting home by an hour. I had been monitoring Oliver's activity for weeks. It was all I could do to keep it inside and watch it all unfold. I am the type of person that typically confronts someone right away. I cannot just let things sit, but I felt I had to in order to get enough proof of his wrongdoing.

Oliver had actually sent me a rare email a day before our anniversary trip telling me how sexy I was and how he couldn't wait for our trip, and yet he'd sent Jena one five minutes prior to the email he sent to me telling her that he was going to be out of town for the weekend, that he would miss her, and how couldn't wait to talk to her when he got back. I couldn't believe what I was seeing. Oliver had been so hurt when he'd found out that his first wife had kissed another woman while they were married. I couldn't fathom that he would ever do this to me. I had trusted that he'd take care of me. He'd told me many times that he would protect my heart. We were supposed to both be starting over in life. How could he know I'd given up being with my own children to stay with him and then turn around and do this to me? I was at a fork-in-the-road again. I could stay or I could go. I felt like a failure in every way possible. I was incredibly hurt, I felt stuck in the situation (fear ruled me), and I had a lot of anger inside of me.

I will never forget the day I came home with the envelope of evidence and told Oliver that we had to talk. He said, "Ok" in a bewildered tone, and I point-blank asked him how long "it" had been going on. He looked like he had no clue what I was talking about. It only served to fan the flames of the anger that burned within me. I told him I knew about Jena. I also told him I knew he'd still been doing porn and even worse, manipulating it to make his own personal portfolio of people he actually knew in real life. He denied it. I *immediately* took the opportunity to drop the envelope on him. He didn't open it, so I did and I began reading the emails between him and Jena that I'd printed. He said he didn't want to hear them. I told him that was too bad, because I did want him to hear them. I read some of them out loud, crying and flaring in anger the whole time. He sat there with a stone-cold look on his face, saying nothing. He showed no emotion at all. I swear, the man was like a robot. I showed him pages and pages of the porn surfing he was doing while he was supposed to be at work. I showed him the grotesque hard-core pornography he'd saved to his computer, and the pictures he'd manipulated himself using pictures from the unsuspecting women that thought they were taking innocent pictures with a friend. Exploitation of the very people he supposedly had long-term friendships with for years. He never batted an eye.

When I got done with it all, I threw it on the table and cried in such anguish I think it actually scared him. It was a groaning of pain like I have never expressed before, and he didn't know what to do with it. He stared at me like he didn't know who I was anymore. I hurt so bad that I felt like my head would explode. At first, he tried to say it was all a set up to see if I was checking up on him. I wasn't about to play the game that led to me being the fall guy again. With everything I had in my hands in black and white, he had no other choice. He finally admitted what he'd done. But as usual, he said that he'd only been "playing a game" and that he didn't intend on leaving me or having an affair. I didn't believe him. I saw their plans in their emails and I wasn't buying it. I didn't feel like I would ever believe anything he told me ever again. I told Oliver not to make contact with Jena again and that it all had to stop, and that if he and Gayle were going to be friends, he was not to see her outside of dropping off his deliveries. He then told me he'd only had lunch with her one time. Another lie, even while caught red-handed in lies. He had lots of excuses and I talked and cried until I had no more energy or tears left in me and I went to soak in the tub.

Oliver wasted no time calling Jena and letting her know I was onto them. In the days after the confrontation, Oliver and I had nothing much to say to each other. I was done asking a liar questions. I decided if I wanted the truth, I would have to chase it down another way. I went straight to Jena. Oliver had actually called and checked up on her the day after our confrontation in spite of me saying he wasn't to contact her, because she didn't show up for work the day after he told her I knew everything. He wanted to know why. She supposedly was afraid I'd come to his workplace and confront her. It killed me every day after that to watch him go to work, where Jena would be right in his face every day. I hurt so much inside about it all that I just went numb. I never felt so much void in my life. I think my soul went numb. I tried calling and emailing Jena several times and she was clearly avoiding me. No response. I wasn't willing to take no response for an answer anymore.

Finally, I left her a message that left her no choice but to talk to me. I was not about to let it go. I told her that my fight was not with her, and that I was only out for the truth which I certainly would not get from Oliver. I told her if she didn't talk to me, I would come to the workplace and tell the boss everything that had happened between them and show him that they were passing emails from their work addresses too. I had the proof and wasn't afraid to use it. She finally got back with me and sang like a bird. She told me that they had been talking to each other for several months. She insisted that nothing physical had ever actually happened and that it was mostly a fantasy world, but she also admitted that they had talked several times about meeting up. She told me that Oliver told her I was not intimate with him, which was entirely untrue. He told her I was abusive. He told her I wouldn't talk. I was so angry I wanted to retaliate, but I had what I needed; the fact was that it was not all a set up to catch me spying on him and that he had been actively pursuing this young woman. I also talked to his friend Gayle, and she told me they'd had one-on-one lunches as friends the whole eight years we'd been married. He had lied that entire time. Not only had he lied, but he had thwarted me of having any friends of my own. I couldn't have any friends; male or female, without him making me feel incredibly guilty. He convinced me through manipulation to isolate myself, and the whole while he was doing whatever he wanted to do. I couldn't even go to church that whole time without him making comments about me running off when I could be doing something with him. It was easier for me not to go, to keep peace. With the truth staring me dead cold in the face, I could have left right then and saved myself more pain, but I didn't. This was a fork that could offer me freedom or more pain, and unfortunately, I chose more pain and I did it all in the name of love. I loved the man more than I loved myself. I decided to try to work it out, even though he refused to go to counseling. Things were so confusing for me after the blow up with Oliver. Part of me couldn't stand him. Part of me was hurting. Part of me felt like an idiot, but there was also a part of me that still loved this man so much I just wanted to fix it all. I thought maybe he needed some time to "grow up". He was eight years older than me! He was in his mid- forties! I wondered if he was going through mid- life crisis or something and hoped it would just pass.

Oliver must have felt very guilty for it all. He flipped on me and all of the sudden he was very concerned and the doting husband again. He held me when I cried, and he cried with me for the pain I was going through, however I never truly saw the kind of remorse one should have when you have injured someone to the core of their being. It all felt so fake. I never got the kind of heartfelt apology I would expect from someone who loves you and knows they hurt you.

It didn't take long for the "old Oliver" to show up again. He got cocky. He seemed to not care anymore. He was acting very cold and distant towards me. I now understand narcissism and how it is switched on and off like a light switch in some people. I tried to talk to him and got absolutely nowhere. It felt like I was back to square one. Oliver said he was done talking about these things and he constantly accused me of trying to stir up trouble. He even got to a point where he would mock me whenever I would cry. Literally make fun of me in my pain. He'd copy me and dramatically act out what I was feeling and saying. I can still vividly remember those times today. He would fake cry and tell me I was acting like a spoiled brat that just wants her own way. I was hurting with the worst kind of pain, and I didn't know how to make it stop. Once he got done mocking me, the silent treatment returned. He would say hurtful things to me. He was avoiding me again. He refused to be intimate with me for months on end several different times, and yet he was still on his porn websites doing his thing. He never stopped engaging in those kinds of activities. He never stopped playing "Dr. Jekyll and Mr. Hyde" with me either. I was forever at the mercy of his volatile moods, and he could flip on a dime.

Recognizing the Wrong Direction

Once Oliver's friend Gayle got the whole story, her heart made a connection with mine. She'd been through some pretty hard times in her life too. Gayle actually became a good friend to me, somewhat of a confidant, and shared a book by Melody Beattie called "The Language of Letting Go" (I highly recommend this book. It changed my way of thinking and helped me change my life).

Gayle was there for me as long as she could be, but she finally got worn out with the drama because I was not doing anything about it. I chose to stay in the situation, and she sort of dropped off the radar. I was a little angry at her anyway, because after I told him not to see her one-on-one anymore he met up with her again anyway. She was going to give him some Bible verses about husbands, which he used to twist against me in the most warped ways you can imagine. It didn't really matter anymore, because I was tired of talking anyway. There was nothing new to tell her or anyone else. It was the same old thing over and over again like a broken record. I did look her up after it was all over to let her know that I appreciated her words; that made me stronger, and for sharing the book. I felt like a hamster on a wheel to nowhere. I went on like that for almost five more years. Up and down we'd go like we were on a see-saw, and I actually got good at pinpointing when he would be the "good" Oliver and when the "mean" Oliver would show up.

The fights and words became so brutal that I absolutely went completely numb. Words that should have torn me up didn't even faze me anymore, I didn't even flinch, and it was scary. Oliver was so condescending. I think I had hurt so badly for so long, I couldn't even feel the pain of things that should crush my heart into a million pieces.

Oliver was always making me feel like our marital problems were *all* my fault. He always had a knack for turning things around on people. I saw him do it not only to me, but to many others, including the ones closest to him. But according to him, *I* had made him this way.

I began looking up information on domestic abuse, emotional abuse, and narcissism. I began to ask myself: Was I being abused? I kept looking up all of the signs of abuse and yet I was still praying for my marriage to be saved at the same time. Let me tell you something; if you have to ask if you are being emotionally abused, then you already know the answer! YES, you likely are living in an abusive relationship! If you will turn your Bible to 1 Corinthians Chapter 13 and read about the truest form of love you will know beyond the shadow of a doubt whether what you have is love or not! Someone who inflicts constant pain upon you does not love you! It is one thing to make a bad decision and correct it, but it's entirely something else to keep doing things that destroy a person emotionally.

Oliver failed me so many times. I had two separate deaths in my family during that time and he didn't go back home to Tennessee with me or support me in any way other than to just drop me off at the airport. He never called. He never checked on me. It should have dawned on me over and over again during our marriage that this guy really didn't "love" me. The same way Faith without Works is dead, Love without Action is dead. At that point, Oliver was being nasty to me no matter what, so I decided I needed to get back to my roots. I needed to find a church, and I decided to go to one right down the road where the boys and I had attended a few times during their summer visits. Thank God those boys had asked me to go! I ran into the warmest group of women there. I now had a support system, though I didn't really talk much about my marriage with the group. Rather, I confided in one mainly. What I did find there was strength, and some sense of comfort. I also started engaging more with the girls from work in an occasional lunch, or home visit.

I found comfort in a special lady from church that I'll call "Meredith", who was there for me every step of the way, encouraging me to see my own self-worth and change the way I was living. I'd promoted at work several times over twelve years at work and by now had a nice income. I had the power, yet fear had kept me stuck in the same old vicious cycle for many years. It was mostly the fear of regret. I didn't want the burden of having failed another marriage. I didn't want to have gone through all of those years believing in my marriage only to add another failure.

Oliver didn't like the fact that I was actually interacting with people occasionally. He was not fond of the fact that I was going to church regularly either. He would act depressed sometimes and other times he would just be flat angry. He threw tantrums. He tried to manipulate me constantly into feeling guilty. He'd follow me to the church sometimes and show up in the ladies' class to see if I was where I said I'd be. It was so strange. I got better at not reacting to his favorite tactics anymore. He was still doing porn as much as ever, and still rejecting me as a wife intimately and emotionally.

I was growing stronger spiritually and emotionally and I finally matured to a place that if he was going to give me the silent treatment or act like he wanted nothing to do with me; I was going to go where someone wanted me around! I also decided to start taking steps toward a better life. One way I did this was to go purchase a small item for my "future life" every time Oliver would treat me like he didn't care about me. I still have my very first purchase; a four-piece set of small bowls. It is still a symbol to me today of the day that I finally said "no more" and made small efforts to take steps towards a better life. I cannot tell you what triggered it, other than to say everyone has his or her own limitations of what they can take, and the closer I got to God, the stronger I became. I had to feel like I had done everything in my power to save my marriage, and I could honestly say I had. My conscience was clear, and I wasn't going to be Oliver's emotional punching bag anymore.

One night I tried to get Oliver to explain to me why he'd rejected me every way possible. I wanted to know, so that I didn't repeat those bad calls again. I never wanted to go through that type of rejection again in this lifetime. As usual, he refused, telling me that I'd most likely never know why. I told him not to wait until it was over, because by then I wouldn't care anymore. He basically said it was the way I treated him and made him feel, but he would give no examples or explanations.

I was tired of feeling like I was sharing my husband with women online, and I told Oliver he had to choose between his porn and me. I was not going to sit back and watch him look at other women in ways he wouldn't even look at me, especially when he was refusing any kind of intimacy with me. He told me his choice was porn and that he doubted he'd ever stop. I guess he thought I was just talking again and wouldn't follow through. After all, we'd had these conversations before, and in the end, I was still there. What were the consequences? I was always erasing my "line in the sand" to let him run right over my emotional boundaries. I had to own that responsibility. I told him I wasn't going to put up with it anymore, and Oliver's response was that I needed to go file for divorce. I told him I didn't have any money, so he angrily wrote me a check and told me to make it happen, "tomorrow"! He'd done this sort of thing and said those kinds of things to me many times before because he knew it inflicted a *lot* of pain. I'd end up begging to stay every time, but not this time! I printed off the paperwork for a divorce and filed it the next day just like he told me to.

I felt like a robot that day. I couldn't believe I walked into that court house and did it, but unlike the few times I'd left before and come back, this time I didn't feel that overwhelming regret. I felt I'd done what I didn't really want to have to do, but was absolutely necessary to do to save whatever pieces that were left of "me". I didn't even cry after leaving the court house when I filed the paperwork. It seemed like a dream. I had no idea what would happen next, but I knew anything was better than the way I'd been living. One of my favorite things I began to say to myself was, "I can do *bad* all by myself", and I still believe that is true!

When I told him it was done, he said, "I would have never had the heart to do that to you!" I guess he forgot writing the check and demanding that I do it. I guess he forgot that he'd said his pornography was more important to him. I guess he forgot the many things he'd done with no remorse at all for years to lead us to that point. After many emotional rounds of "whose fault is it" sessions, it turned out all he was really worried about is the responsibility of paying half of my debts and me taking the dog I'd adopted from a shelter. I had taken care of the animal in every way getting up in the middle of the night when he was a baby to take him out and taking care of his medical needs to buying his food, but somehow Oliver loved the dog more than me. This man was more worried about a dog than the fact he was losing his wife. In fact, he shed not one tear during the whole process about our marriage, but he wept uncontrollably over that dog. With the divorce almost final, I made plans to return home to Tennessee. My boys were grown now and my mother was getting older, and I felt it was time to be closer to my family. It was so scary to leave a secure job, and the only place I'd known for fourteen years. It was hard to leave my church. It was hard to leave friends behind, but I felt a pull to go back home to the place I was born and raised. I needed to be closer to my kids.

When my CEO learned that I was trying to get back home, he set me up with a severance package to help me get back home and I cashed out my 401K savings. In this way, God had made a way for me to survive while I was looking for a job. He was giving me a way out of the desert. I rented and furnished a house when I got back to Tennessee with that money and lived on the rest for 7 months. I was still hurting very badly over the death of my marriage, the fact that I wouldn't see my step-daughters much anymore, and the time I lost with my kids by trying to survive in a situation that was doomed from the beginning.

On Again Off Again

After only a few months back in Tennessee, Oliver and I began talking again and we agreed to try to work things out even after a divorce. Another fork- in-the-road with a neon sign: Which path would I take? I truly loved Oliver regardless of what he'd put me through. I went against my better judgment for that one last shot to fix it. I sold everything in my house that I'd just managed to secure and went back to Phoenix. It left everyone shaking their heads (including mine) and fearing for my sanity and my safety. Before I ever left, I warned him that I would not go through the same old routines. I meant it too. I went with an open mind, but a guarded heart.

It was weird to be back in Oliver's house to say the least. It was right at Christmas time. The girls and Oliver exchanged gifts; however, I was not allowed to participate. He had always been like that during holidays, but now it was even more painful for me. He'd used his girls as a weapon against me many times. He'd say he was going to take them out or do something with them and I was not invited. He knew I couldn't just go pick up or see my boys anytime I wanted to, so it was the perfect weapon indeed. I was so much closer to my boys when I was in Tennessee and could have spent Christmas with **them**. Was he really going to try this with me? I had told Oliver that I would not do any of the old stuff. I was not about to have the same arguments, fight, or live the way we did before, and if we were starting over that meant he had to stop behaving aggressive towards me and treating me like an outsider. Oliver had changed the code to the garage door when I'd left for Tennessee after the divorce, and he had no intentions of giving it to me now. He'd always been controlling in a manipulative kind of way, and now he had even bigger reasons to "make me pay". I had a house key, but my car now sat outside when it had always been parked in the garage during our marriage. One night it all came to a head and I asked him why he'd told me he wanted to work it out, when it felt like all he wanted to do is bring me out and punish me in some morbid way. It ended up in yet another battle, and he ended it with telling me that he didn't feel the same about me anymore, and that he'd probably never be intimate with me again. He said he would probably never give up his porn, and that things were going to be a lot different this time. He said he was not going to let me be close to him or the girls for a very, very long time because he would not let me damage all of them too (being the damaged person I was). What was different about this? He'd driven a wedge between me and the girls before and he knew it was an effective way to isolate me and to hurt me. This was not new at all.

    Oliver went to bed, locked the door to the bedroom behind him, and I knew that he would not be speaking to me the next day. Those last words he said would be the last words I would be there to hear him say to me; "I don't feel the same about you anymore." It tore me up, and I felt like the dumbest person walking God's green Earth. I'd just sold everything I owned and spent fifteen hundred dollars to get back to him, only for him to burn me again. Now I'd have to spend another fifteen hundred just to get back home, and my money was disappearing with every month that passed. My mind was made up this time. I had to stick to my guns and that meant I could not let him do this to me. I would not go through this anymore. I would not continue to play the mind games. It was time to draw my line in the sand, and to mean it! I now realize how stupid it is to continue to do the same things over and over with someone and expect to get a different outcome. I cried until I couldn't cry anymore. I was so upset I knew not to try to drive in that condition. I remember getting to a place that night that I literally couldn't feel anything at all. It was like every part of who I was got sucked out of me and the carcass was cast aside much like a spider does its prey.

As soon as Oliver left for work the next morning, I loaded up my car with the totes that I never even unpacked again (like I must have known it was coming), and I took my little Willie dog and headed back East for good. A co-worker who'd become a sort of mentor and friend called me and gave me a basket full of snacks and things for my trip, and it was then I started thinking about the kindness one person shows for another and what that actually looks like, versus the alternative.

Time to Turn Around for Good

When I got back to Tennessee, I was running low on funds. It had been six months since I'd worked. It was taking a while to find a job and I was in panic mode, and feeling lost and rejected. I had to go live with my biological father for seven or eight months, and thank God, he welcomed me with open arms. It gave me time to spend getting to know a dad that never really was in my life until I became a young adult, and **this** time he was there for me in a big way.

I reconnected with the friends I'd grown up with and people who had been cheering me on towards a better life. I was finally closer to my children too, and I couldn't wait to see them again. I soon found a good job. I'd been looking before for months unsuccessfully. I also ran into a guy I went to school with in the meantime who'd been through his own tragic story and we began dating mostly as friends to distract ourselves from the pain, and it was nice to have someone to talk to that could relate to what I was feeling. I actually was scheming to hook him up with a friend of mine who'd been through a rough relationship and divorce, BUT…half a year later, we were married. Something happened, and we became more than just friends. I can't believe I ran into him almost no sooner than I made the decision to make a permanent change in my life, and stop being a victim. I said I would not get married ever again. God sent me someone that could truly love me and who really **needed** me too, and didn't mind saying it. I had given up on love. My husband and I have mutual respect for each other. We go to church together. There is no hostility in our home. I got a new opportunity to build a relationship with my grown children, and I hope to be a much better grandmother someday than I was a mother.

Life is looking much better than before. Strangely, once I decided I was not going to continue in a life where I couldn't be the best person I could be, things fell right into place in a way that blows my mind. It was only after I made a firm decision and stopped doing the same old things that I got a reprieve. It was the most painful lesson I could have learned. It's about respect. It's about loving yourself. It's about boundaries that you do not let anyone cross. It's about your relationship with God. It's about so many things. I could go on and on, because I learned so many lessons through those years of pain.

My sole purpose for writing this book and "airing out my dirty laundry" is to help someone that may be on the rocky paths I've trod. It is my desire to help someone think through the pain that is keeping them "stuck". It is my desire to help you rise above the pain and learn to love yourself. The truth is; you are never really stuck unless you choose to be. For every fork-in-the-road, you get a choice. Each and every one of us was born with the God-given gift of free will. That free will is going to take you to forks-in-the-road where *you* make choices (God will not force his will upon you), and those choices send the dominoes falling down a particular path that very moment. It's up to you to write your own life story. Even fairytales have adversity in them. How can you know victory if you haven't known adversity? It's what you do with those adversities that really matter. Dr. Martin Luther King, Jr. said, "The ultimate measure of a man is not where he stands in moments of comfort and convenience, but where he stands at times of challenge and controversy". I hold that quote so very close to my heart. The question is, what are you made of? How bad do you want a better life, and who do you want to be?

When faced with adversity, you have two choices: You can lie down and die, or you can put one foot in front of the other until you find a way out. One thing is for certain; you won't move forward until you are willing to take that first step and the *first* step is the hardest!

Final Thoughts

I would like to take the time to share with you, the most important things (**final thoughts**) that I've learned in my journey:

1. *WHEN APPROACHING A FORK-IN- THE ROAD, CHOOSE YOUR PATH WISELY!*

Life is full of forks-in-the-road, and as previously mentioned, I don't believe either choice is really a mistake. It was a choice. What I know is that I could have saved myself a lot of pain had I chosen a little more wisely. Several of the times that I had choices to make, I knew in my heart that I was choosing a dark, winding path. I wanted what I wanted and I stubbornly walked the thorny path. Sometimes we get what we think we wanted. Some lessons are much more painful than others. If you feel a tug in your heart to go a certain way, know that choosing the other path can inflict years of pain beyond your wildest imagination. This pain may not affect only you, but those attached to you as well. Once you take that first step, you send the dominoes of life falling into a specific pattern that will go until the end of that fork is reached. There is no way to know how long the lesson will last. It largely depends on **you**! Think it all through, and for the sake of all that is Holy… Consider others!

Most importantly:
Pray for guidance and be willing to listen not just to what you want to hear, but to what is in your best interest. God has a perfect plan for your life (Jeremiah 29:11). However, even God gives us free will to do right or wrong. Next time you ask why someone did something so terrible to hurt

you, think about that. The same way you get to make choices, so do they, and once again; those decisions can affect others! Maybe they have a lesson to learn as well. You don't have to be a willing participant!

Trust that God's plan is the best plan. It's easier to walk on a beaten path than a crooked, thorny, winding road. I know that for a fact, because I've tried it. God's presence in my life is the only way I made it through the experiences I faced. Don't blame God if you choose the rocky incline instead of where he tried to lead you. He gave you more than once choice.

2. *AS LONG AS YOU PLAY THE PART OF A "VICTIM", YOU WILL BE!*

Don't participate in another person's pain, anger, or drama to the point you become a perpetual victim. That is his/her journey, not yours. They have to work it out for themselves. You cannot "fix" people nor "make them see what's important". What's important to you at any given stage of your life might not be as important to the next person. Maybe you already took that class in the Hard School of Knocks, and maybe it's someone else's turn.

Stop making excuses for allowing people to treat you badly. They are not "just having a bad day". If they are treating you with anything other than respect, it is because you allow them to get away with it and they can. It took me a long time to realize that I was just as responsible for the chaos in my life as anyone else, because I was a willing participant by not being willing to enforce boundaries to protect myself. My excuses for the reasons I stayed were: "I love him", "I've invested too much time in this marriage", "I don't want to have another failed marriage", "I won't be able to survive financially", "I deserve this" and the list went

on and on. These are all lies we tell ourselves to avoid having to do something to change it. You can confide in, talk to, cry, pray, and agonize all you want; but until you are willing to take a huge leap of faith and **do** something about your situation then you will remain in that situation. Stop looking for someone else to "save you" and save yourself. I was always waiting on someone else to "save" me from the pain in my life. I honestly believe that's exactly why the path I chose led me to the place I went. God had to let me go to that dark place. I learned something valuable there. I learned that if at any given moment in life you don't have family or friends to go to, if no one understands you, or if there's no one who can be there for you in the wee hours of the morning when your heart is full of anguish and agony: **ALL YOU NEED IS GOD!!!!**
"He is our refuge and strength; a very present help in times of trouble." (Bible: Psalms 46:1)
People will fail you, but God will never leave you nor forsake you (*Bible: Deuteronomy 31:6*).

Knowing I had a much higher power at work on my behalf was the only thing that kept me going. Too many times, we put our trust in those around us: mere, mortal human beings. It's important to love yourself as much as you are willing to love others. What would you be telling your best friend if he or she was in your shoes? What would you say to your sister if she were on the receiving end of what you deal with all of the time? Be willing to listen to your own advice, and act on it!

I learned a very painful lesson about boundaries. I've never been good at setting them with people, but that had to change. Example: I started by buying something "for my new life" every time Oliver would do something to hurt me. Even if it's just buying that set of bowls for your "own place", one small step still takes you a step closer to a peaceful life. It shows a desire to make a change. It shows you're willing to take the steps, even if they are small. God will see that you have taken that first step of faith, and he will be there for every step after. The first step is the hardest, but the path doesn't get any easier UNTIL you take it!

3. *DON'T LET FEAR KEEP YOU IN A BAD PLACE.*

Fear is a crippling emotion. I know when I was going through my hardest tribulations; fear is what kept me in the middle of the storm. I was afraid I was making the wrong decisions. I was afraid of what others would think of me. I was afraid I wouldn't be able to financially make it. I was afraid I would later be filled with regret. I was afraid I would hurt or disappoint everyone I loved. I was afraid of change. I was afraid of being all alone. I knew I wanted relief. I knew I wanted peace in my heart. I knew I wanted to be loved. I knew I didn't want to come home every day and wonder if it would be a good day or full of misery. I knew I didn't want to be in pain forever, but I was absolutely terrified of that first step. Have you ever watched a baby trying to learn to walk? They don't just let go and walk.

First, they crawl around, then they begin to pull up on things and stand, then they walk holding onto supports, then they stand alone for a few minutes, then finally they get brave enough to take that first step. I watched my boys hold their breath sometimes for that first or second step. It didn't take long before they were walking all over the place. In the beginning, they were afraid they would fall. They did fall sometimes, but they got back up and tried it again. Life might look really scary to you at times. You might not think you can do it but trust me; you can do it! Even if you fall once or twice, it will not kill you. You get smarter, and you get stronger. Don't beat yourself up if you "chicken out" a time or two. Just don't give up on walking! I have been through more than one trial in life where I was scared silly. I was afraid to make any move whatsoever. Once I got brave enough to do that, I found out that it wasn't as bad as I thought it was going to be. It hurt, but I didn't die. It was very difficult and my whole body, heart, and soul trembled; but somehow whenever I got brave enough to jump into my fear, I ended up landing on my feet. I don't mind saying on a few of those occasions I absolutely do not know how I did it. It had to be God.

Many times, I'd cry myself to sleep wondering how in the world I was going to do it. Odds were not stacked in my favor and I knew it. But I also knew I was a lot stronger than I thought, and that if I put my faith in God, he would not leave me there to die. Sometimes you hold yourself back from a better life simply by being too scared to do anything about your situation. For every day you hesitate, you cheat yourself of a day you could have been living in abundance. Look your worst fears square in the eye, and jump! Your loved ones will be there to cushion your fall. If you don't have loved ones you can depend on, then believe in yourself! If your life has become more pain than joy, what do you have to lose anyway?

You'd be surprised at how once you do that; you will look back once you've made your jump and say, "Wow. That's what I was so afraid of? Why did I not do this for myself long before now? Why did I waste all of that precious time?" Don't waste another second. None of us are promised tomorrow. I didn't want to get to the end of my life and say, "I should have done something". **Today** is your opportunity! My favorite Dr. Phil quote is, "The only thing worse than living in this situation for 10 years is living in this situation for 10 years and one day!"

4. THERE IS NO WAY AROUND THE PAIN. YOU MUST GO STRAIGHT THROUGH IT!

If fear wasn't bad enough, another reason I was unwilling to make a change is because I didn't want to endure the pain. I felt like I'd had enough pain in my life already. The ironic thing is that I was in pain anyway. I was in deep, chronic pain, and I don't know why I thought the pain of leaving a bad situation was going to be more painful than it was to live in it indefinitely. I kept wishing that I could just "fast forward" through the pain, or ignore the problem and thereby avoid having to go through it. Realistically, I knew I couldn't live the way I was living forever and I also knew that along with any change you will experience pain.

I wish I could tell you that getting out of a bad relationship or a bad situation meant that you could end the pain immediately. The truth is; that's impossible. I remember nights where the pain was so bad I'd cry until I had no tears or energy left in my body. Sometimes the pain would engulf me in a way that I couldn't cry at all. I finally reached a conclusion that I had two choices. I could take a flying leap of faith and leave the situation and hurt for a little while or stay in the situation and hurt potentially for the rest of my life. It took me almost nine years to make a decision to remove myself from the source of the pain, and about twelve to actually remove myself for good, because I loved my husband regardless of the things he did or said. I loved him more than I cared about my own well-being. That is not real love. That is called "co-dependency". Drug addicts like what isn't good for them too and it's just as hard for them to kick the habit as it is for a person who is dependent on other people in a way that they feel they have no self-worth if they are "alone". When I did finally make my decision to leave for that final time, I didn't really feel that much pain. I think it was surreal to me.

Everything seemed strange. It's almost like I was going through the motions, but I wasn't really in my own body. Your soul can only take so much before it begins to shut down. I'd left several times before and I melted down into full blown anxiety attacks, crying spells, hyperventilation, and I dare to say; nervous breakdown. It always led to me running back out of fear. I grieved fiercely when I would try to leave and I felt fear like I'd never felt before, because I feared life without Oliver. When I finally made a firm decision to stop the insanity the dynamics changed.

This time it was different. I felt nothing as I loaded up my car and left Phoenix that day. It would be great if that's where the pain ended, but it didn't. When I began getting closer to the man that is now my husband, I had bouts of anxiety and withdrawal and he had to be very patient with me. I was hurting in my heart still. Every time I get close to someone I get hurt, so I was very reluctant to "touch the hot stove eye again to see if it was on." With time, I was able to release my heart in a way that I could return the feelings he was more than willing to share with me. I guess now you think that because I found love again that the pain stopped? I'm sorry, but that is not the correct answer. It has been years since I went through my divorce from Oliver and if I give myself a minute to think about it, I can easily feel the tears well up ready to spill down my cheeks. I fight them back many times, but sometimes I just let them fall where they may. I hurt because it was not necessary for the marriage to fail. I hurt because I really wanted it to work. I hurt because it could have been prevented. I hurt because I remember the good times, and because I miss my step-daughters who grew up during that twelve-year marriage. It's a different kind of pain now. I know that with time it will subside, but just like a death of a loved one you must go through the same stages of grief with a death of a marriage. There is a part of me that will always feel sadness and just a little bit of pain because of what happened. I couldn't stop it, and for me it was a senseless death of a marriage. What I **can** tell you is that it gets easier to live with, and actual forgiveness can manifest. The kind that frees your soul and spirit.

    I have moved on with my life, and I'm happy now. I am surrounded by the people who love me most. I am at peace for the first time in a very long time. There is no drama or chaos in my life anymore, and it's wonderful! If you hesitate to make a change in your life just to avoid the pain, let me tell you it won't work. You can remain stuck in a terrible kind of pain, or you can move on with pain in your heart to a better place and work on healing that part of you that has been injured. No one else can make it better for you. You can take medications to ease the pain, you can try to drink it away, you can engage in lust of the flesh to feel the void, or you can just avoid it altogether by doing nothing; the choice is yours. But this fact remains: *The only way to make your life better is to decide that you are worth more and take the steps towards a better life.* Take one step at a time even when you don't feel like it; just by putting one foot in front of the other until you can feel yourself coming back and trust me you will find yourself! Act *as if* you're headed to a better place until you get there!

    Avoiding pain will not save you from it. You have to work your way through it, and you will! Doesn't it make more sense to take the path that at least has some potential to lead you to a better life? You have to run towards your most dreaded pain and fear full force. You have to meet it head on, push past it, and set your eyes on that light at the end of the tunnel with full determination to reach it. There is simply no way *around* the pain. You have to walk **right through it**! I promise you that once you do, what is on the other side will be very worth the things you had to go through to get it! I still go through pain in my heart once in a while over the things I've experienced, but I'm still much better than I've ever been!

Don't let pain steal what's left of your life. Get up and fight for it! Take a leap of faith today towards a better life! I began by simply buying a few dishes for my "new life" every time I was emotionally attacked or neglected by my ex-husband. It was my way of doing something more than just talking. It was a signal to me that it was time to take care of myself. It was a symbol of a new life that I gave myself with God's help.

5. *IT'S EASIER TO TALK ABOUT FAITH THAN TO WALK IN IT.*

I was brought up in church. I knew about God and how much he loves us and that if we just believe when we pray; he is faithful and just to answer our prayers. I heard the sermons about "stepping out in faith believing". If you open your Bible and read Matthew 21:22 it says, *"And all things you ask in prayer, believing, you will receive."* That sounds so easy, doesn't it? Well, it's a lot easier to believe and to have faith when things are controllable, but when all seems hopeless; having faith can seem a lot easier said than done. The Bible says that faith is the substance of things hoped for, and the evidence of things not yet seen (Hebrews 11:1). I am here to tell you that when you don't know how you're going to take care of yourself or where you're going to stay it's hard to have enough faith to make your feet move. When I was scared out of my mind and my heart was full of pain and doubt, I would repeat over and over again, "I still trust you, Lord." I don't know why it took me so long to be willing to make a change. I do know that God was with me at my darkest times.

I now know exactly what it means to walk by faith. I had a good friend that told me, "Just jump! Do it!! Everything else will fall into place." I knew that, but terror kept me from taking the plunge for the long time. I'm so glad I did. Once I did, it really did all fall into place. I can tell you that I was holding my breath for sure when I did it. I can also tell you that more than a time or two things have begun to look very bleak and not at all in my favor. But I can also tell you that every time, just in the nick of time, I have been thrown a life-saver. I don't know how it happens. I have no explanation except that when you have that kind of total trust and faith in God, he takes notice and he will be right there! He shines his grace, and sends a life boat your way! Some of my favorite verses in the Bible are found in Matthew 6:28-30.

(28) "And why worry about your clothing? Look at the lilies of the field and how they grow. They don't work or make their clothing, (29) yet Solomon in all his glory was not dressed as beautifully as they are (30) and if God cares so wonderfully for wildflowers that are here today and thrown into the fire tomorrow, he will certainly care for you. Why do you have so little faith?" (NLT)

I finally get it that if I am strong enough to believe just long enough to put my faith to action, God will be there to meet me. I know it's hard not to worry. I have been there

and done that and worried myself sick. It was all for nothing. I was already in misery. I was already scared. The only difference was that once I grew enough faith to just do something, I actually got somewhere!
Before that, I was caught up in a vicious cycle that went absolutely nowhere but to very dark places no one would ever want to be. **Find a support system**! Whether it's a church, or a friend that is willing to encourage you; it's very important to have positive people in your life. There will be time those people may not be able to be there for you. Please know that it's during those times that God wants you to lean only on him. You can trust him, because he cares for you. No one can do this for you. You have to walk it by yourself; no one else can "make you" have faith. It is all up to you, and you can do it! Many have done it before you, and many will do it after you. In the words of my good friend, Gayle, I say to you, "Stand strong!"

6. *FORGIVING IS FOR YOU, NOT THEM.*

Once I got through the hardest part of the pain, it began to bother me that I'd left some loose ends. Oliver and I hadn't said more than a handful of words to each other before I left. There was so much I wanted to say before I left, but I decided that I'd said enough during the whole marriage. What more could I say? Besides, he'd told me he didn't want to hear anything I had to say about it. I had to walk away with no explanations or any answers for "why" things had to end, especially the way it ended. I used to wrestle with it back and forth. I don't so much anymore, because I realize that sometimes you don't get answers. Sometimes people go missing, never to be found again. In this case, a refusal to talk or offer anything that might give you closure or peace can leave you with emptiness inside.

The only advice that I can give you is that you just have to let some things go, and that's hard for someone like me that needs answers to feel at peace with myself. You have to trust that God will help you bear the burden. You may have to find your own peace in knowing you did all you could do. Maybe it's better not to know what the other person thinks. After all, did this person give you peace or comfort while he or she was with you? It's okay if you don't get all of the details. It's not going to kill you. You can still go on and find your own happiness.

Once the dust settled and the pain became manageable, I realized that part of the lingering pain was because I did not make amends. Like it or not, I was in that relationship too and it could not be all one person's responsibility or fault. I don't know what I could have done different, but I'm sure there are things I didn't do right. Regardless of what happened, I needed to forgive Oliver. Forgiving was not about excusing his part in the whole thing. Forgiving was freeing for **me**! It was about starting over with a truly clean slate. I'm sure he did what he thought was the best he could do, and maybe he did do the best he could with whatever tools he had at that point and time.

Maybe the next person will get a totally different Oliver, who knows? I finally sent him a message one day. I told him that he didn't need to be nervous about hearing from me and that the message was not going to be negative, nor a rant of accusations. I told him that there is part of me that will always care about him, and that I'd loved him the best I knew how with everything I had to give and that I hoped someday he could forgive me for the unraveling of our marriage. I told Oliver that I did not blame him for everything that happened, because I realize it takes two people to make a relationship and that I was very sorry for my part in the way the whole thing played out. I told him that I really do hope that he finds someone he can love with all of his heart and that he has a wonderful life. I ended it with, "May blessings follow you and the girls forever", and I meant it. I can't say the pain has completely disappeared forever, but it has become a valuable lesson to me that I know will help me in my life now. I learned a lot about gratitude, and about the love we should have for each other. Forgiving has helped me clear a path in my soul so that I can live the best possible life I can life, and I can also forgive myself and push the doubts I have about myself being just bad at relationships altogether further from my mind. I am freer to love the way I need to love. I am free to hold my head up high knowing I made amends in my own way. I don't need the answers to everything anymore. I don't need him to validate his part in the demise of our marriage. I just need healing of the heart and mind, and I am on my way. To forgive the person that hurt you is not a favor to them. Forgiving those that hurt you is about granting yourself peace and the freedom to shake the dust of the past off your feet.

Forgiveness is a gift you give **yourself**. Speaking of forgiveness, it's important to forgive yourself too. You are only a human, bound to make a few bad decisions. Learn from the experience and move forward. If we were made to look behind us all the time (like in the past), we would have been born with our heads screwed on in the opposite direction!

7. *BELIEVE THAT GOOD THINGS ARE COMING AND YOU ARE WORTHY!*

After a second failed marriage, and all of the crazy things I've been through, experienced, and done it was hard to believe that good things could be just around the corner. I was so used to things falling apart and wandering off of the beaten path that I was just not prepared for what happened next. From the ashes of a broken life, I began to crawl. I had looked for a job for seven months, and just when I thought I was going to be washed down the river I was given a good job with great benefits not very far from where I live. I thought I was going to be alone for a very long time and unable to share my heart with anyone, but God sent me a very loving, Christian man that goes out of his way every day to let me know how valuable I am to him and how much he loves me. I worried about having to live with my dad forever, yet God gave us beautiful place to live. Sometimes my husband and I struggle with the same daily challenges everyone has, but we are happy and that's worth a lot more than money can buy. I had been separated from my children by fifteen hundred miles for a very long time; There is much less distance between us now and I'm very happy that I'm able to see them more. Where there was nothing but tears and sorrow in my heart, there is now laughter. Where there was loneliness, there is love. I finally realized that if God can forgive me for all of my failures, and send his son to die for me, then I can learn to accept the pardon Christ bought with his blood.

    Still, while good things were happening, I sometimes found myself waiting on the other shoe to fall. If I'd only known that it was just a matter of me believing and stepping out into grace, I might not have been so scared. Human beings are amazing creatures. Created in God's likeness, we have the ability to survive against the greatest odds. Our hearts can be broken into a million pieces, yet we can still be capable of love. We can stand in the shadow of death, and still have a smile or a song in our hearts, while we persevere even when the cards are stacked against us. We can be hanging by a thread and despite our circumstances; we can still possess something called "hope". Don't ever underestimate the power of God. Don't ever underestimate the power you possess inside! Regardless of what you may be facing right now, or what you've been through; I am going to ask you to believe. Believe in yourself. Believe in the power of prayer. Believe in the grace and mercy of God. Believe there is an answer to every problem if you just have the faith to find the answer. Most importantly believe that you are exactly where you're supposed to be at any given moment in time. Your choice at the fork-in-the-road may have taken you where you are, you may be where you are for someone else to learn a specific lesson, or you may have followed someone else down an unfamiliar path in error; but God knows where you are at all times, and he knows where you are supposed to be and if you ask him, he will re-direct your path! The hardest thing is timing. God has perfect timing, and his timing doesn't always coincide with *my* timing! If you take a close look at your past, I'm sure you will see several times when a situation had you wondering what in the world you were going to do, but somehow you lived to tell about it! You may be going through a terrible storm right now, but as my Pawpaw once told me: A calm always comes at the end of a storm, and after it's all over you just might see a rainbow! Take a deep breath, trust in your journey, and know that good things (sooner or later) will come your way! Have a little faith!

    I would like to close by saying; I hope that I have given you some insightful things to think about. I hope you know that no matter what choices you might have made in life when you came to your very own forks-in-the-road; you are still very special to God. He still loves you! I hope you know that you are valuable and that you most certainly do have a purpose. He had one for you before you were ever born! Whatever your circumstances or what you may have done, you are worthy of all of the good things this life has to offer. We are all here on this Earth living our lives the best way we know how. Along with that come inevitable growing pains. Be kind to yourself. Be forgiving towards others. Know that you are human, and as a human being you are not expected to be perfect. **I don't ever want to forget where I've been or what I've learned, because that's how I know where you don't want to go (again)!** Use what you've learned to become the best person you can be. Drill it into your thinking that you are worth so much more than a chaotic, painful life. God doesn't want that for you any more than you'd want that for your own children. Don't let someone that you allowed into your life to make you feel like trash. Remember, you were wonderfully and beautifully made with a purpose and a perfect plan for you in mind (Jeremiah 29:11-Holy Bible). Lastly and most importantly, please know that there's nothing, *absolutely nothing* that can separate you from the love of God! Not EVER! Therefore, you are never alone, and in his arms, you will always find love!

"(38) For I am convinced that neither death nor life, neither angels nor demons, neither the present, the future, nor any powers, (39) neither height nor depth, nor anything else in all creation, will be able to separate us from the love of God that is in Christ Jesus our Lord." ~Holy Bible (NIV-Book of Romans)

PERSONAL NOTE:

If you haven't received Christ as your personal savior, I invite you to do that today. It will change your life forever! All you have to do is believe that He died for your sins, ask forgiveness for them, invite Him into your heart, and follow Him for the rest of your days. That's not to say that you'll never face challenges again, but you will have someone that loves you so much that you'll never have to feel alone again. I am so thankful I had the knowledge that no matter what; if I turned back from my "wicked ways"; a loving, merciful, and forgiving God would be waiting with open arms to rescue me from my wreckage. I would have never made it, if not for the faith that had been instilled in me from a very young age, in a God that loves with an everlasting love. It doesn't hurt to give Him a chance. If you already know who Jesus is, but just wandered away, it's never too late for a U-turn! Wherever you are in your life right now, may God's peace go with you on your journey; may He surround you in His love; and may you find yourself living an abundant life with a heart full of joy. May you rise up from the ashes and start over with brand-new hope for your future, and a chance for something far better. I know you can do it, because I am living proof that it's possible!

Tracey ♡

Author contact: all.about.trcy@gmail.com

www.ingramcontent.com/pod-product-compliance
Lightning Source LLC
LaVergne TN
LVHW010302260326
834688LV00044B/1414